OTHER BOOKS BY LAURIE SALZLER

POSITIVE LIGHTNING
IN THE STILLNESS OF DAWN
A KISS BEFORE DAWN
RIGHT OUT OF NOWHERE
AFTER A TIME

EYE OF THE BEHOLDER

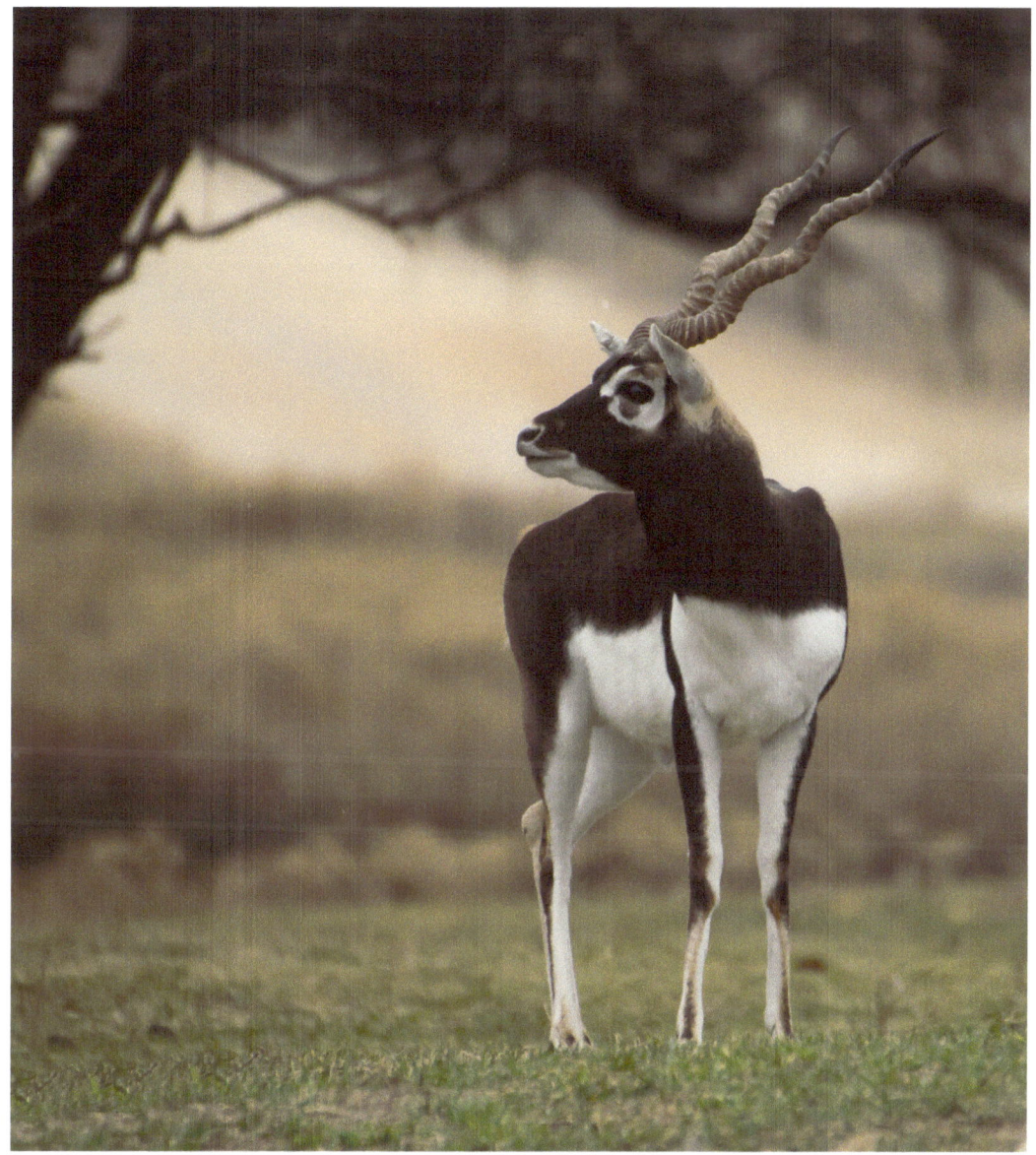

LAURIE SALZLER, PHOTOGRAPHS • SHEILA PEARSONS, TEXT

Bink Books
Bedazzled Ink Publishing Company • Fairfield, California

© 2016 Laurie Salzler
© 2016 Sheila Pearsons

All rights reserved. No part of this publication may be reproduced or transmitted in any means, electronic or mechanical, without permission in writing from the publisher.

Deluxe Edition

978-1-943837-25-0 deluxe paperback
978-1-943837-24-3 paperback

Cover Design by

LS DESIGNS

Bink Books
a division of
Bedazzled Ink Publishing, LLC
Fairfield, California
http://www.bedazzledink.com

ACKNOWLEDGMENTS

Laurie Salzler

The one thing I wish I could add to my photos is sound. For then the picture would truly be complete, for you would see what I see and hear what I hear. Pictures appeal to one sense and I see that as a downfall. The only way I can enhance them is to add words that touch the soul. Sheila, your words enhance every single photo within these pages. Thank you for accompanying me on this journey. Most importantly, thank you for being one of the best friends I could ask for

Casey & Claudia from Bedazzled Ink, you're awesome. Thank you for everything you do to make this photographer and author happy.

To the people in my life who've given me the encouragement and strength to continue, every single one of you is bound to my heart by a silver thread.

Sheila Pearsons

Photographs always focus and reflect the instant taken. Laurie Salzler's images do that very well, but they also offer. They offer a way of seeing, they offer a sense of place and perspective, and they offer the opportunity for views held to expand. Good photography is as much about the heart as it is about the eye. Laurie, to have my words echo your vision has given me great pleasure. For the opportunity and the encouragement, and most of all for being my friend-I thank you, Authographer!

With much appreciation to the people who have taken time to read my meanderings, and who have commented, "liked" or otherwise offered support, your generosity and kind words mean much. And to several close friends who have long been encouraging readers, sincere thanks. For much patience and ongoing kindnesses, thank you E.

*Shadowed clouds both reflect and portend the day's dawn,
filled with opportunity and color—ready.
Perhaps in the shadows is where dreams live.*

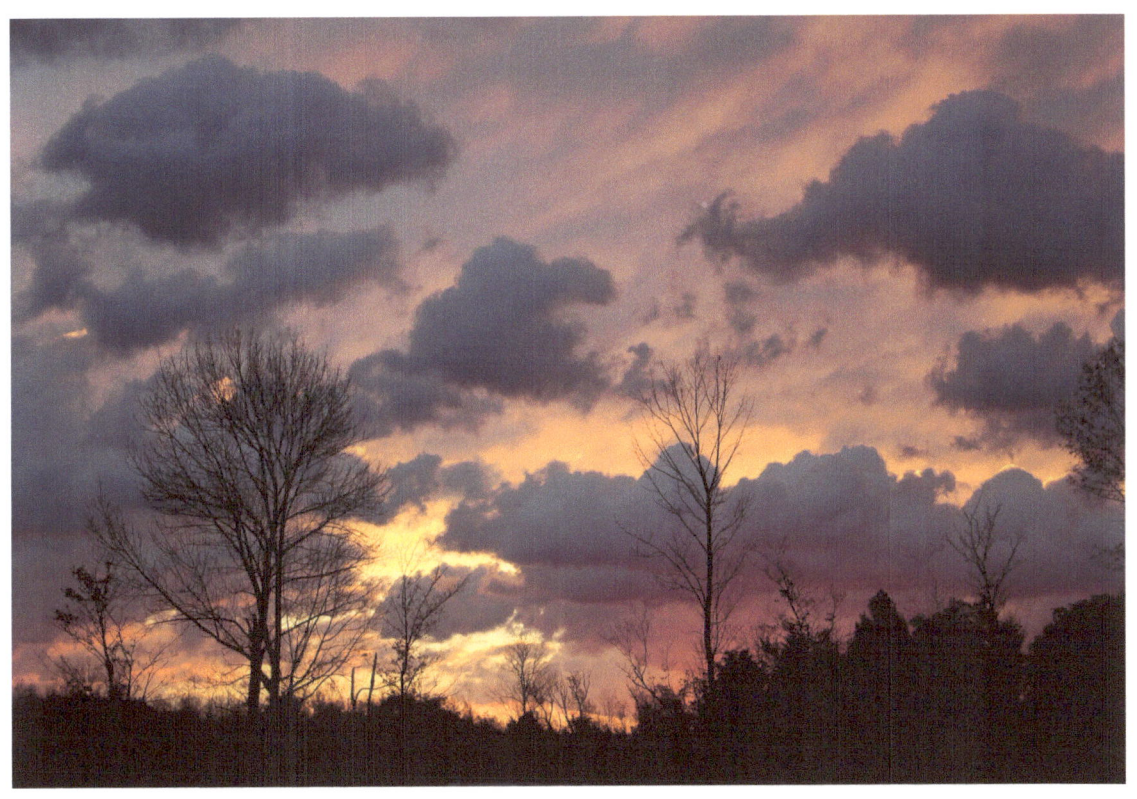

Derby, New York

With quiet strength, power and determination in perseverance, standing solid and facing the wind, overcoming odds against, this is Tenacious Tatanka.

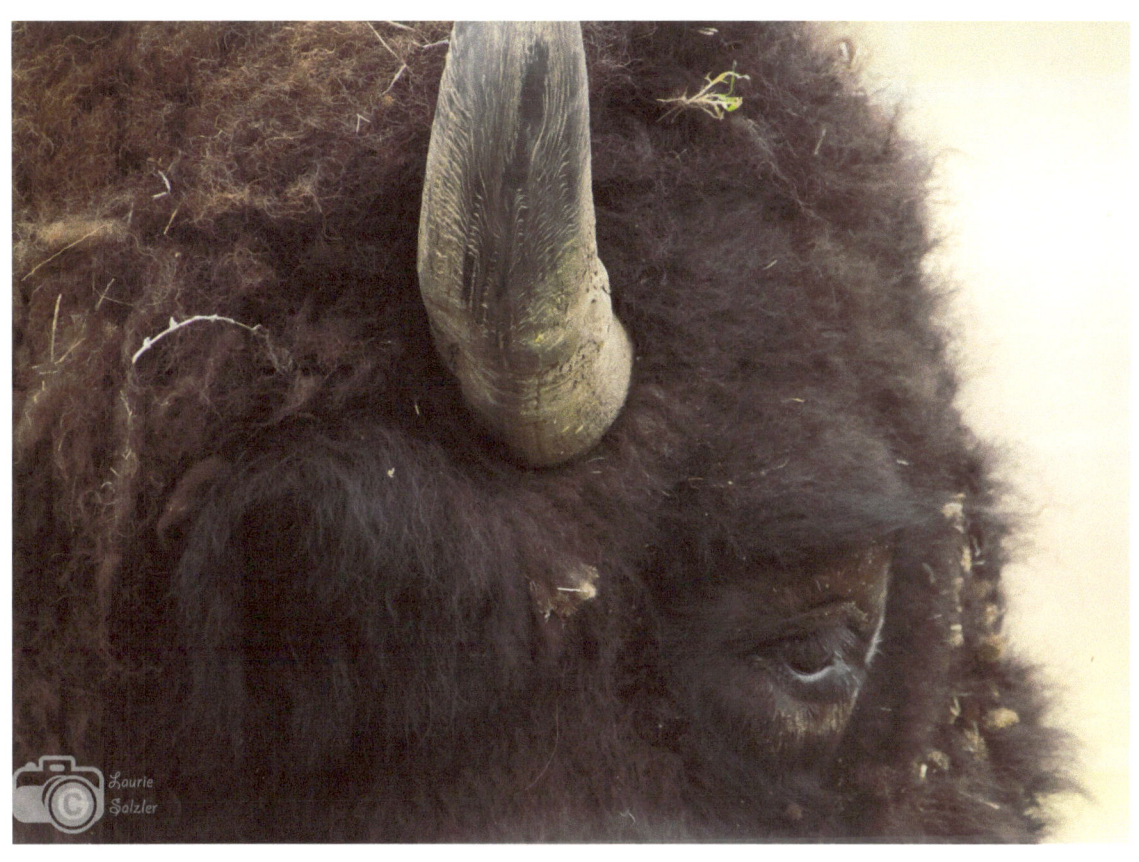

American Bison
Fossil Rim, Texas

*As if floating and silent,
the calm water reflects a peaceful coexistence.*

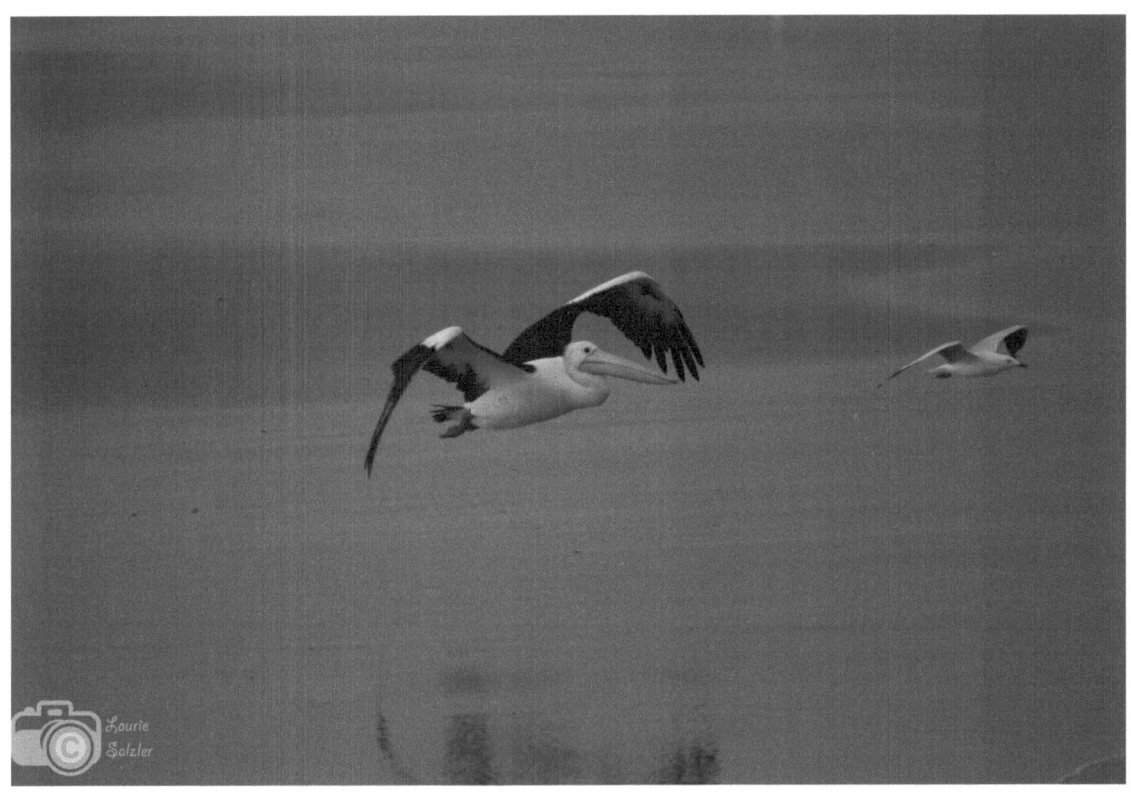

Australian Pelican & Silver Gull
NSW, Australia

*Watchful and aware,
the kingfisher waits and the branch becomes vibrant.*

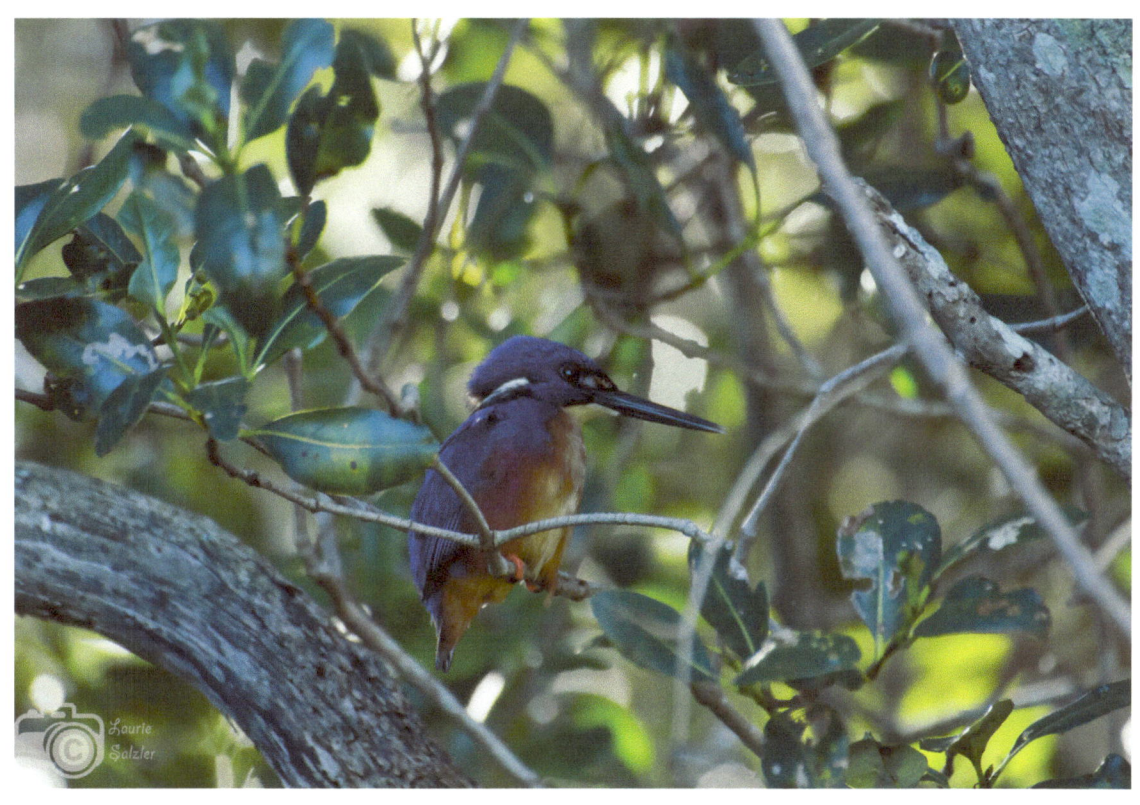

Azure Kingfisher
Chatsworth Island, NSW, Australia

Knowing where to stand and covering the territory, there seems to be a controlled formality and an eagerness.

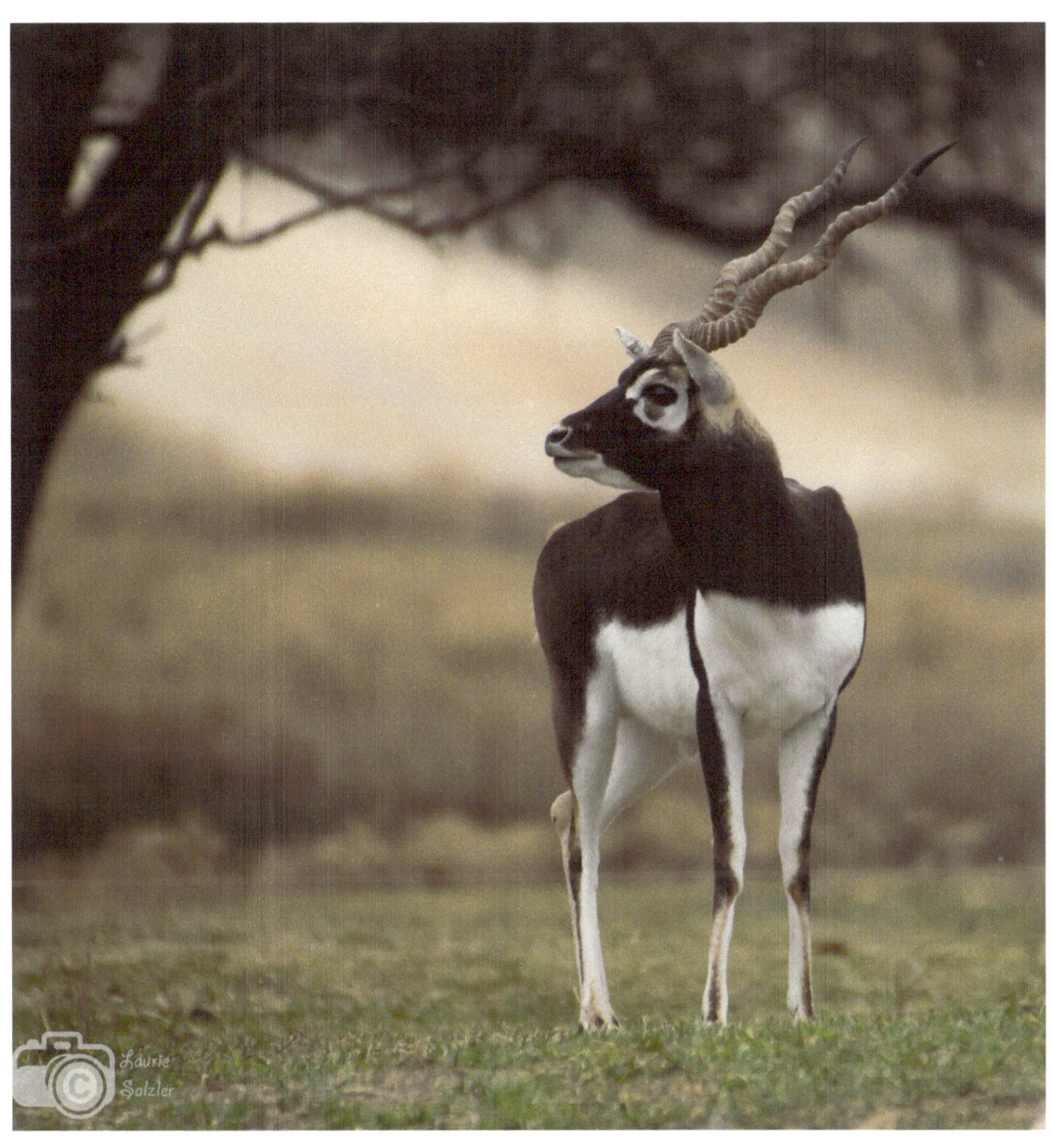

Blackbuck
Fossil Rim, Texas

Loud and raucous,

Jays' consistent sightings in a seasonless year—

they are always present and brash.

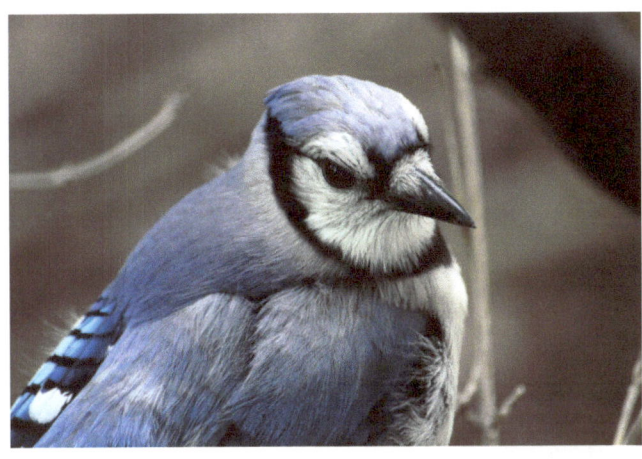
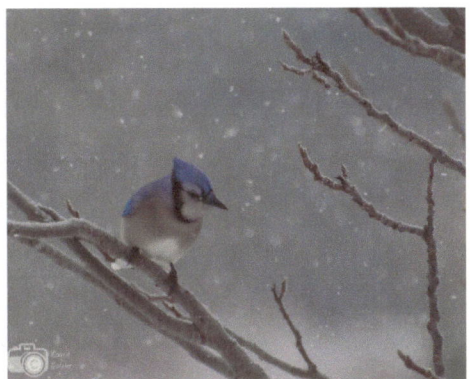

Blue Jay

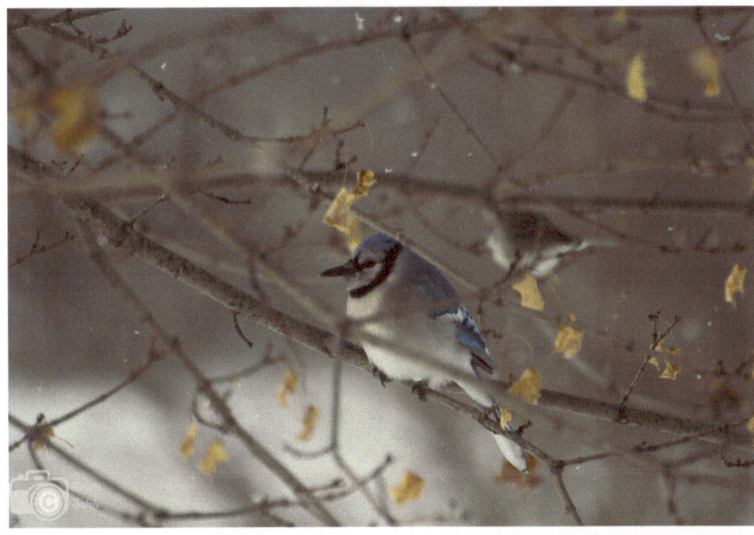
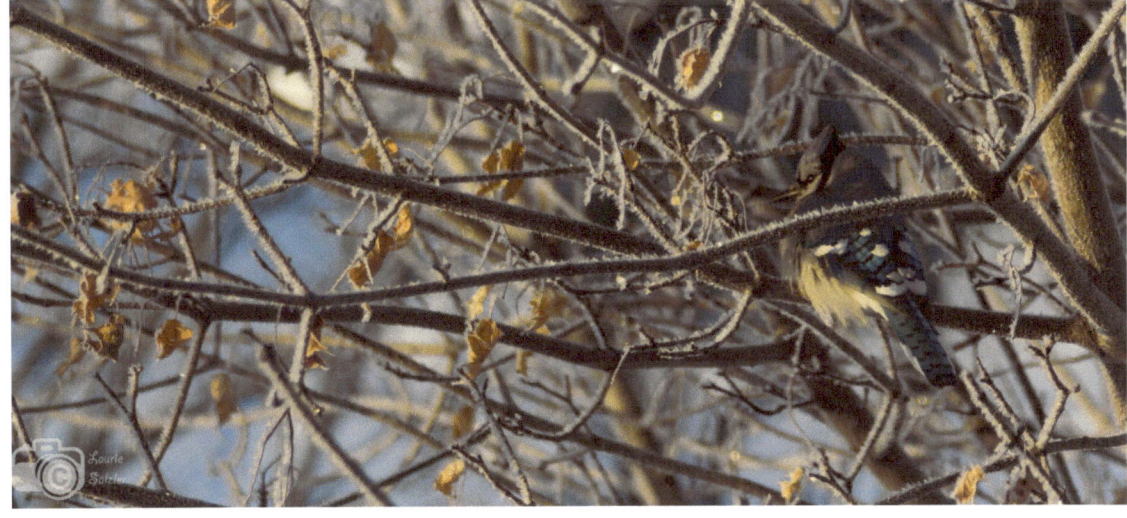

Looking awkward and disproportionate,

yet steady—

equilibrium is impeccable at feeding time.

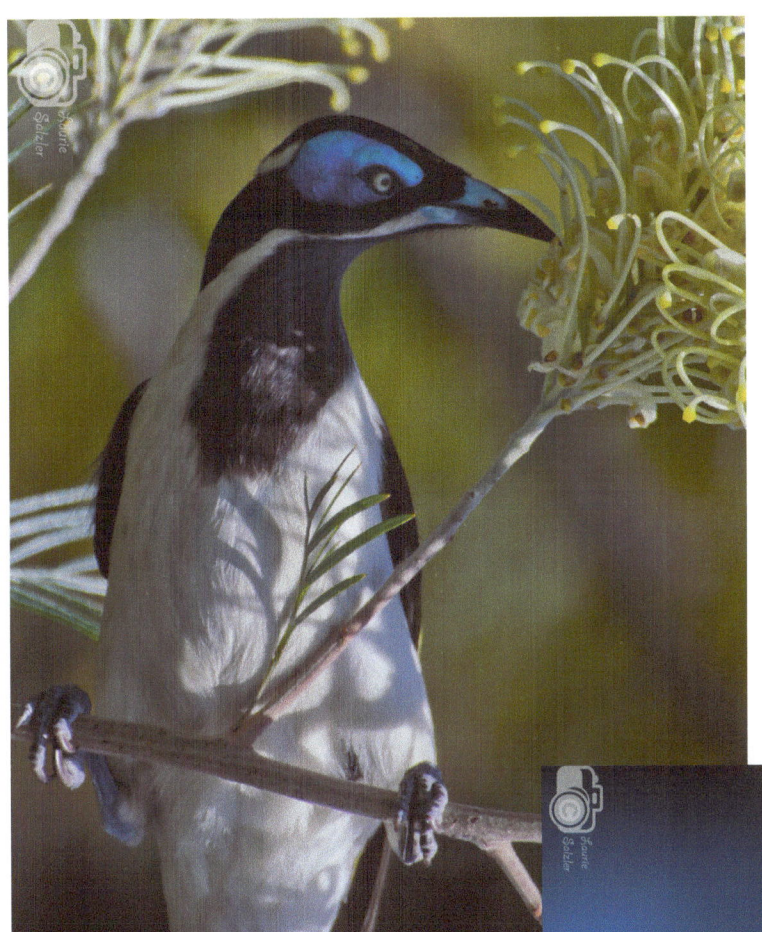

Blue-faced Honeyeater
Ashby, NSW, Australia

With poised reaching,
the achieved goal tastes all the sweeter—
wings as balance pole on the tightrope branch.

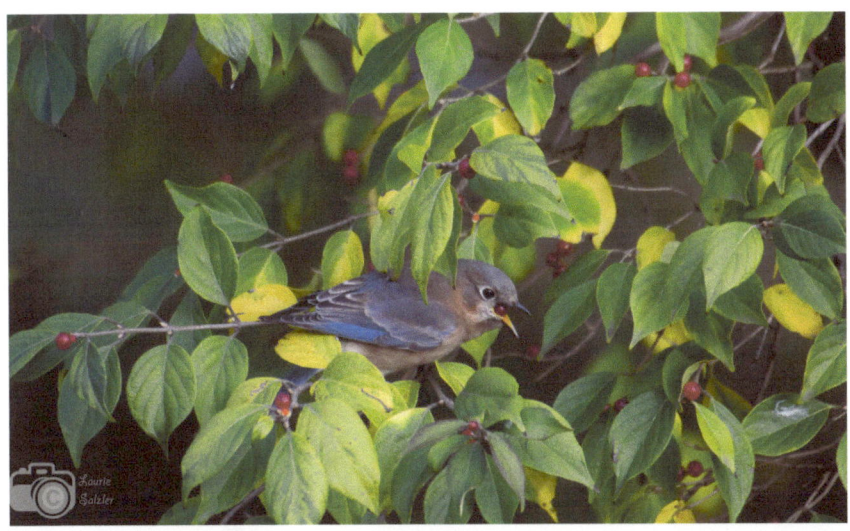

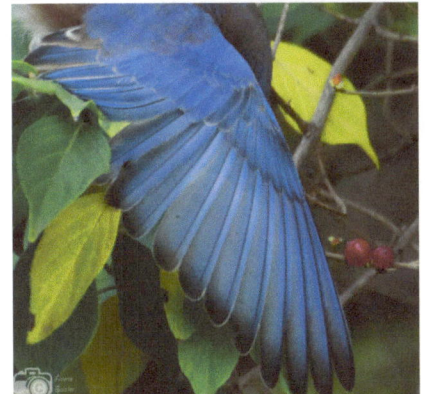
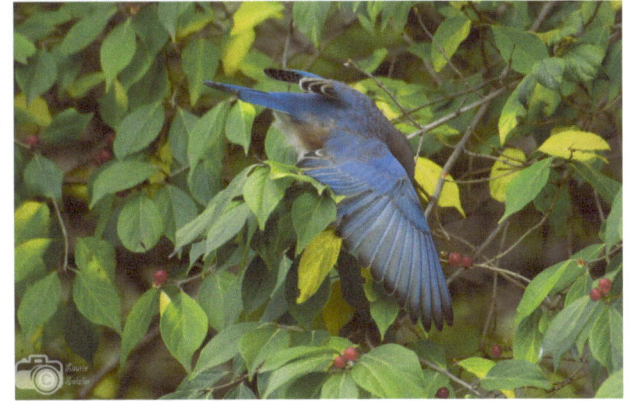

Eastern Bluebird

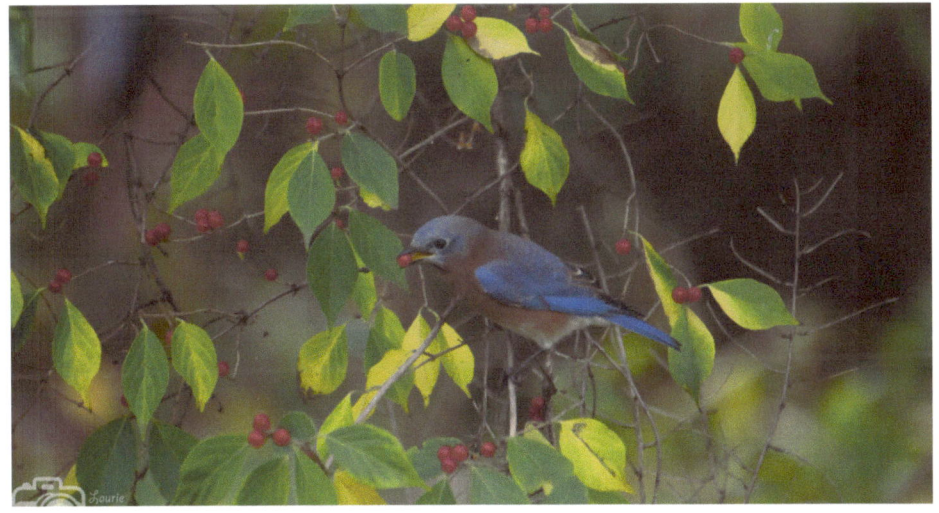

With recognizing the unusual in the common,
a humble quiet intensity is revealed.
Let us always be astounded by quiet, modest beauty.

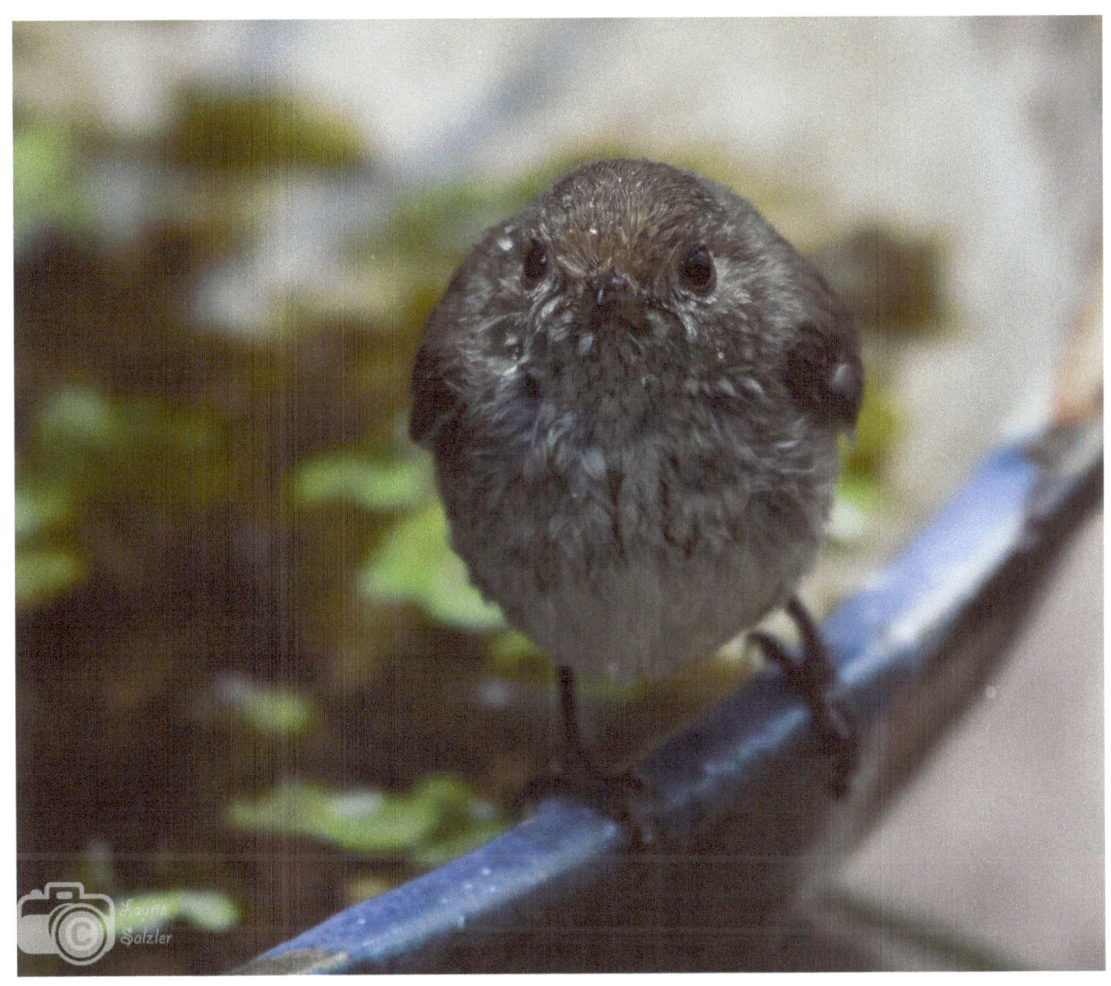

Brown Thornbill
Ashby, NSW, Australia

*Crimson avian burgee arrives,
igniting the tree with flames of energy,
repositioning the arcs of focus.*

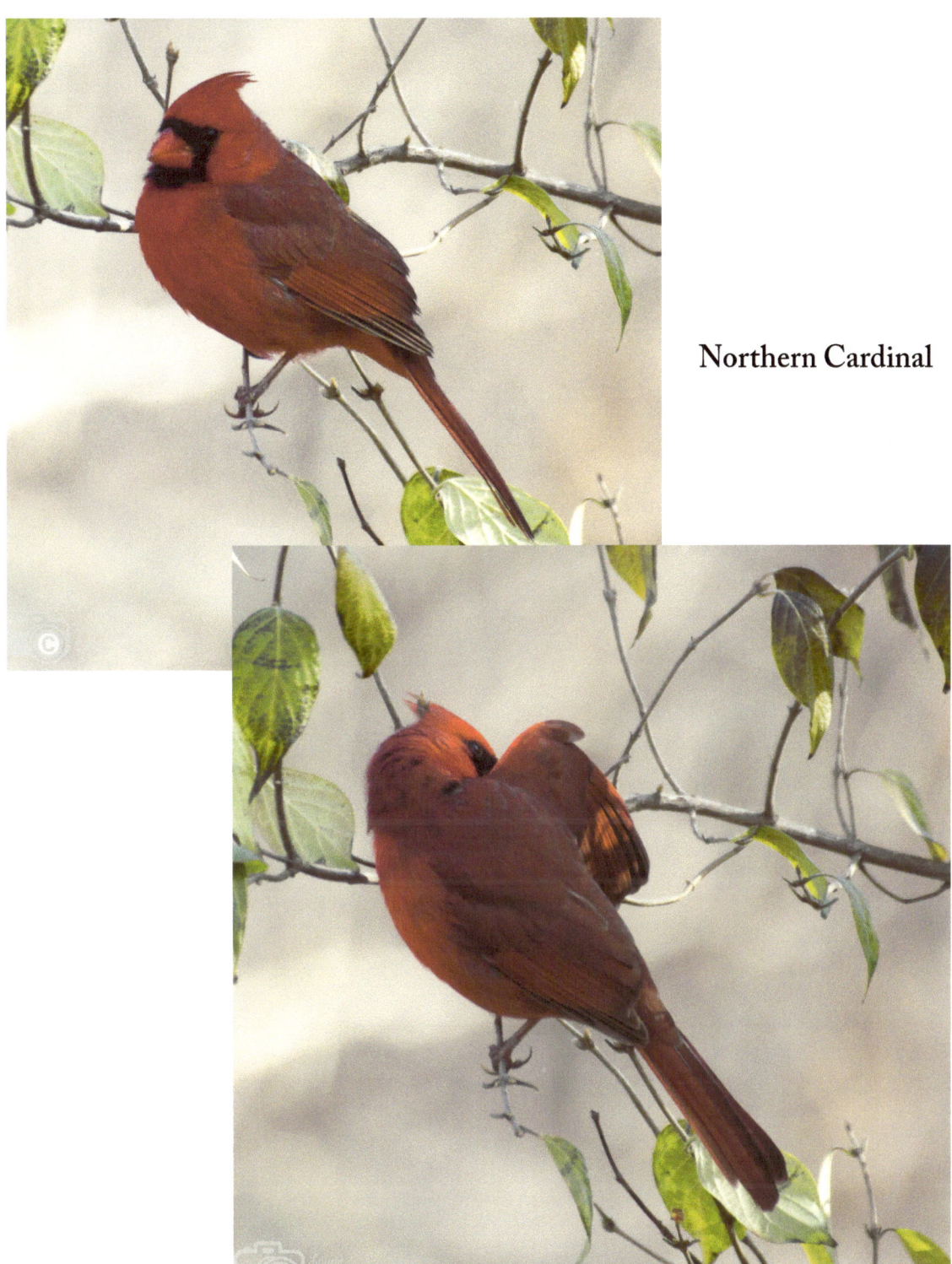

Northern Cardinal

Backlit clouds over the Clarence,

quiet and calm before the day,

wakes of movement and life.

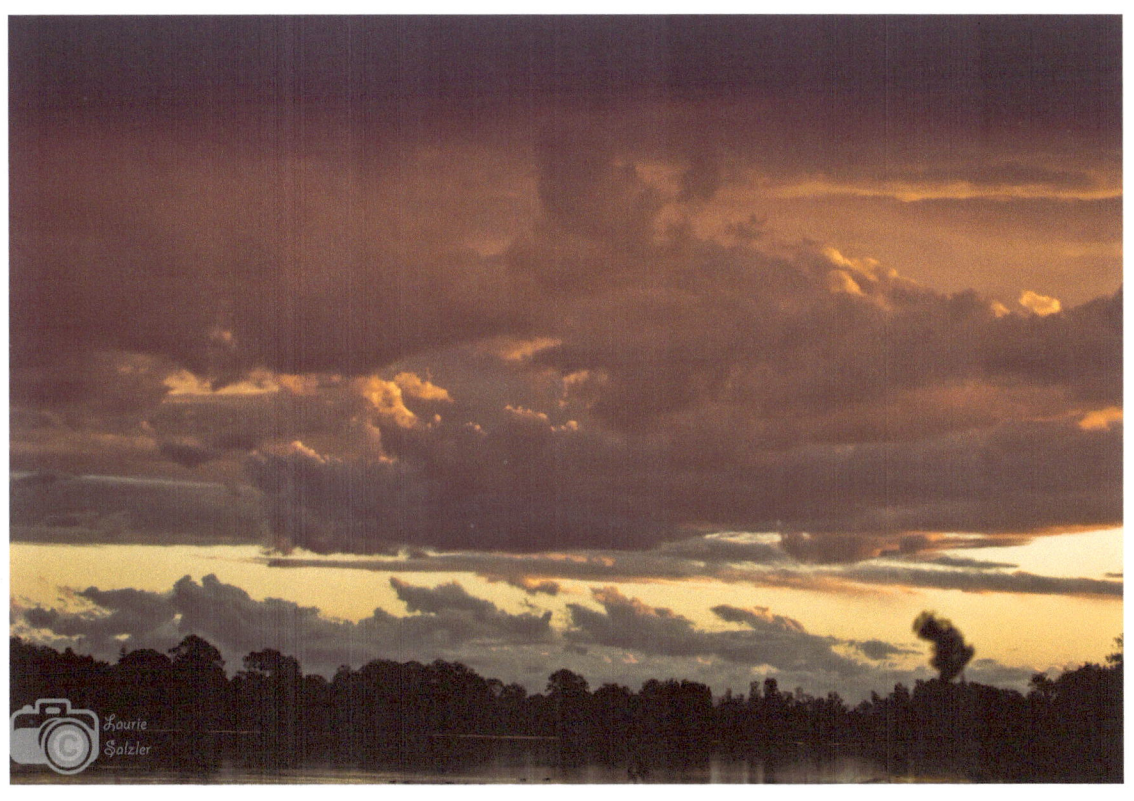

Clarence River
Ashby, NSW, Australia

The bend of weathered strength hangs and hovers

preceding the storm,

casting shadows below the sun.

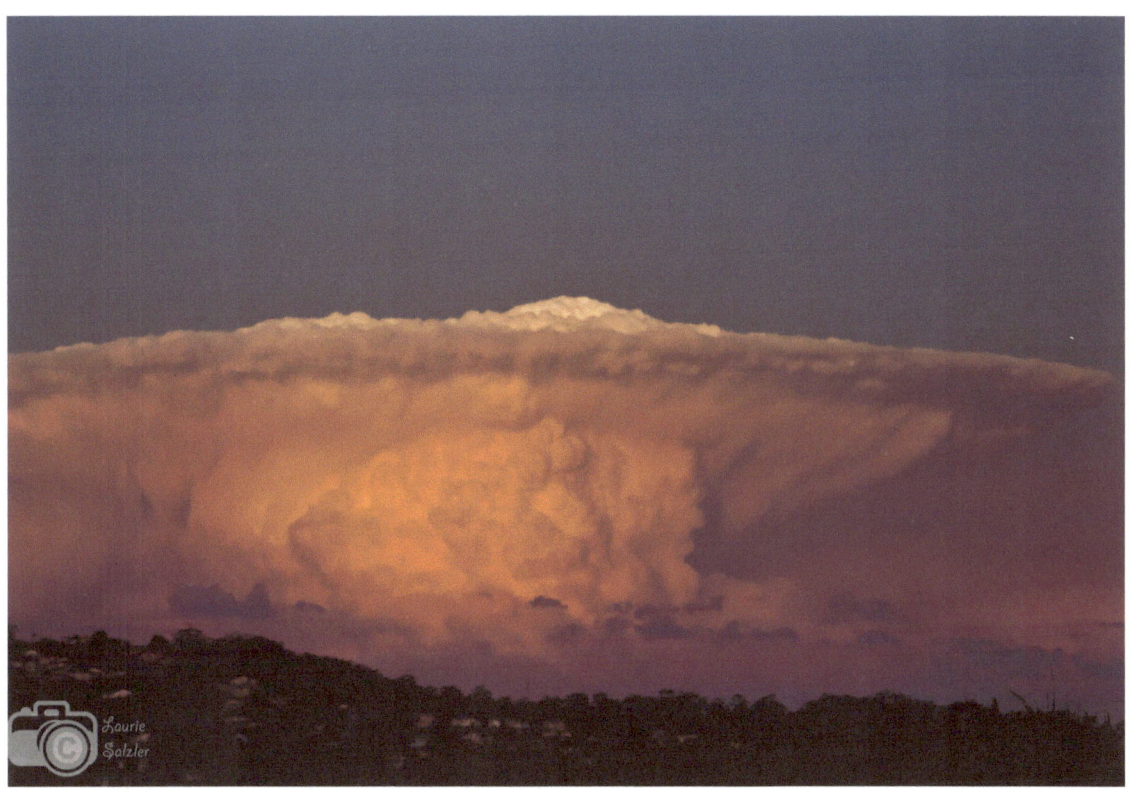

Maclean, NSW, Australia

Making way toward the water,

purposeful flight silhouetted against the golden sky,

grace-filled, measured line moving . . .

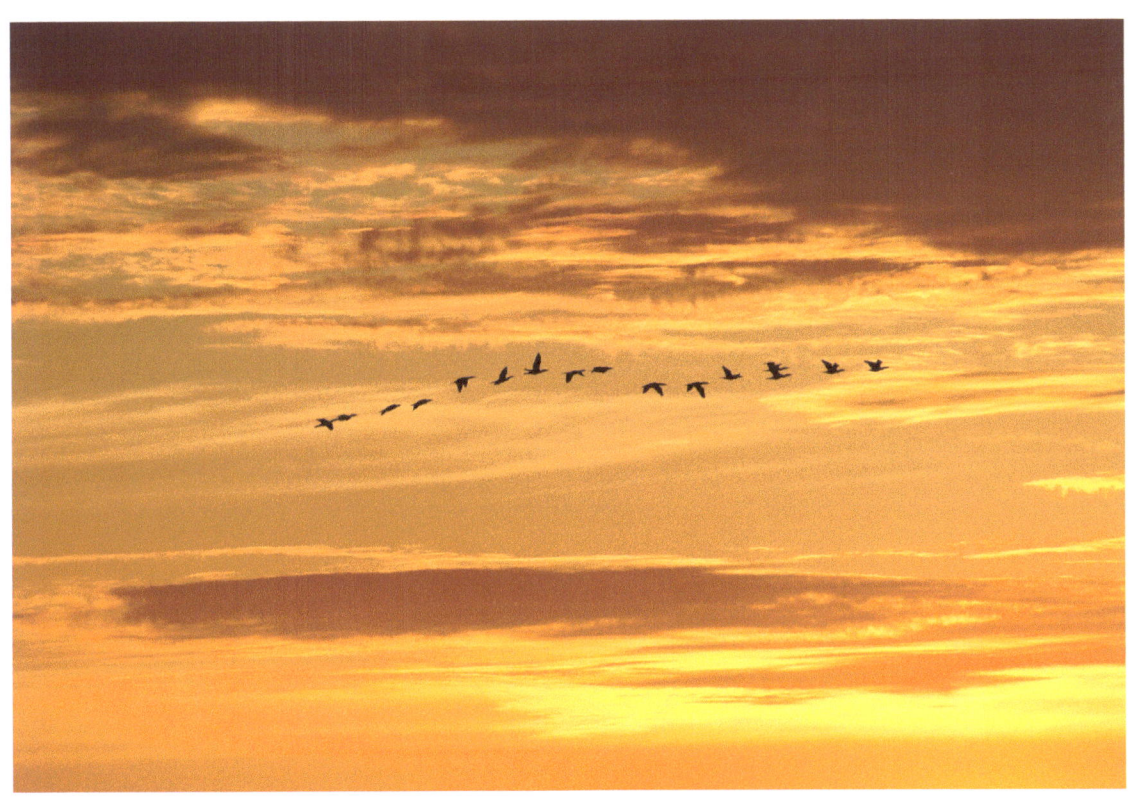

Cormorants
NSW, Australia

Dipping to meet the evening,

the vespers of this day

settling into night bring calm and peace.

Eye of the Beholder 33

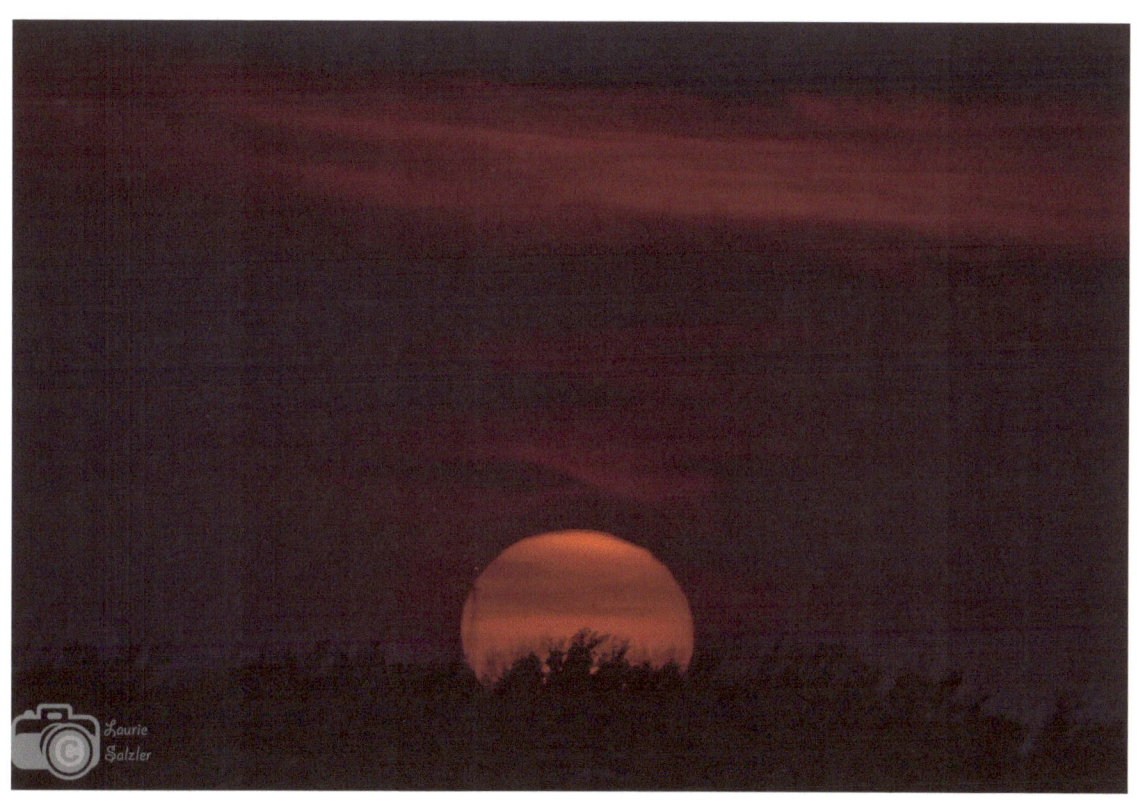

Dallas, Texas

Though the colors' camouflage lessens the risk, attentive and intense observation is required, diligence saves.

Eye of the Beholder 35

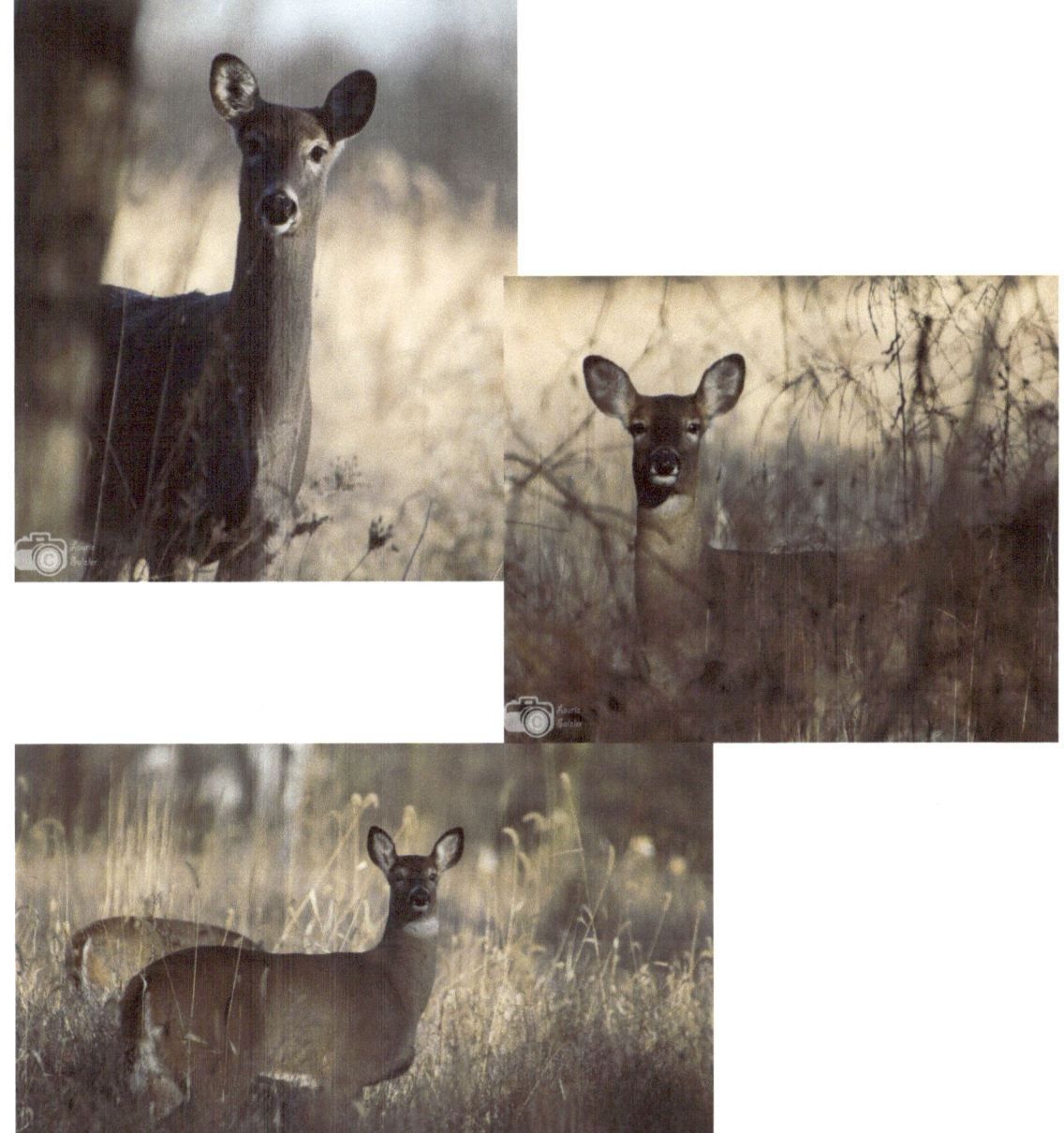

White-tailed Deer

Surfing the crests, in play there is freedom.
Joyfully swimming together, individually and in unison,
the pod echoes the movement of the ceaseless waves and foaming surf.

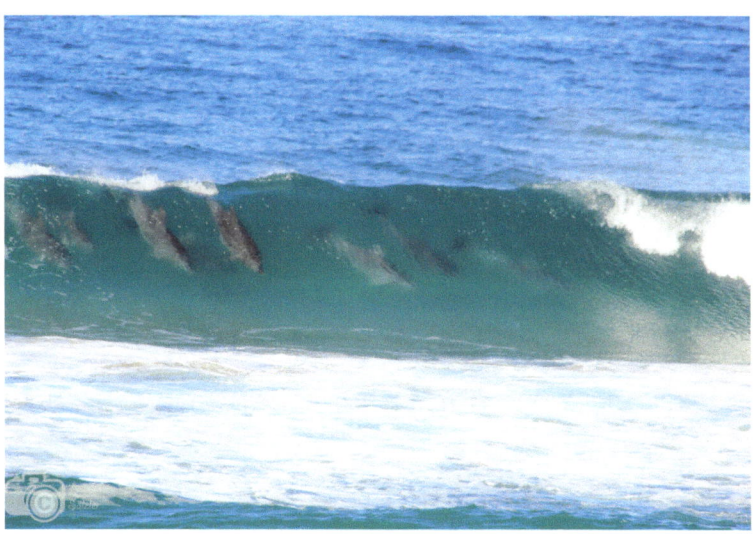

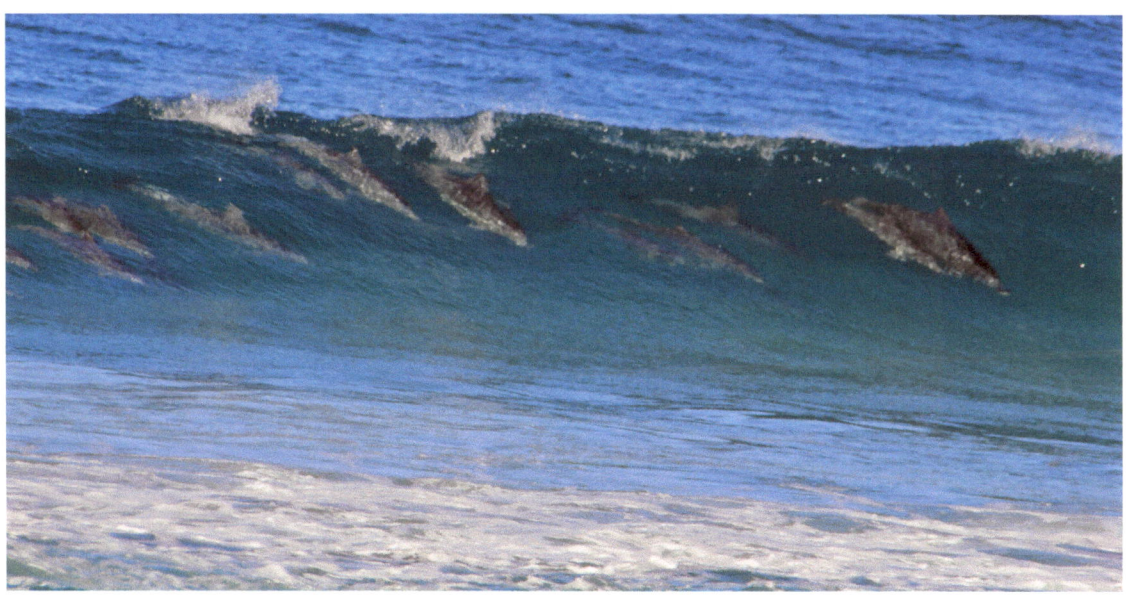

Dolphins
Yamba, NSW, Australia

*Quizzically disheveled and inherently comical,
there is a sweet innocence and delight that shows in an honest grin,
belying the committed stare.*

Eye of the Beholder 39

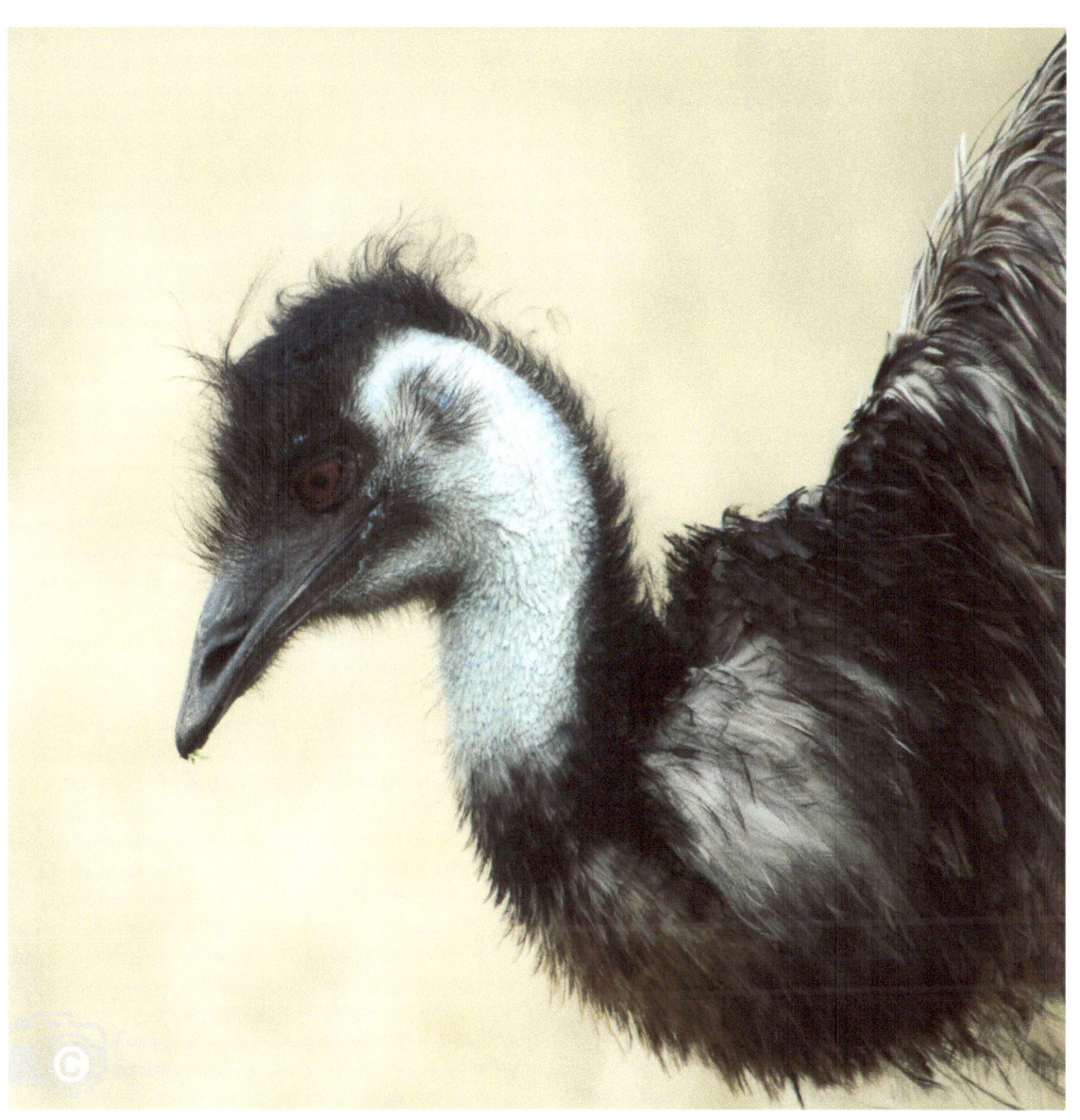

Coastal Emu
Brooms Head, NSW, Australia

In simplicity and nature's grand scheme, there is a common thread of connection, always connection.

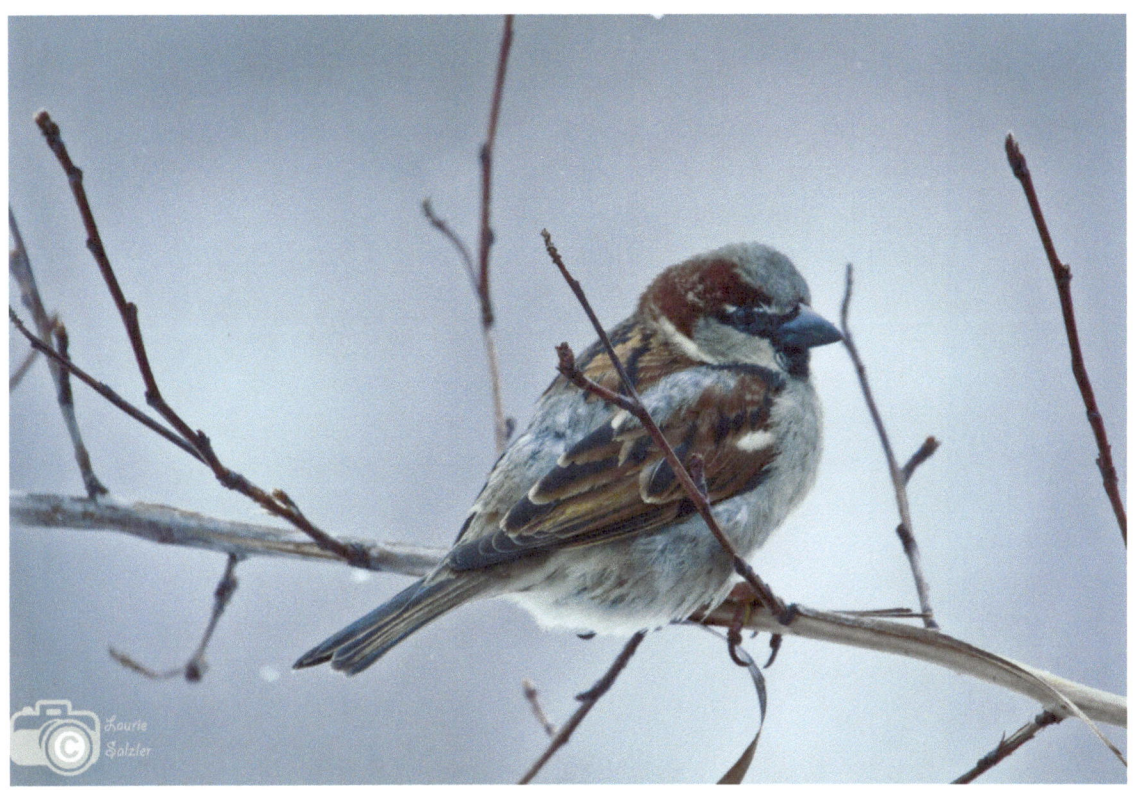

English Sparrow

With the gray of nonchalance, and a familiar call,

there are choices of standing out,

or blending in.

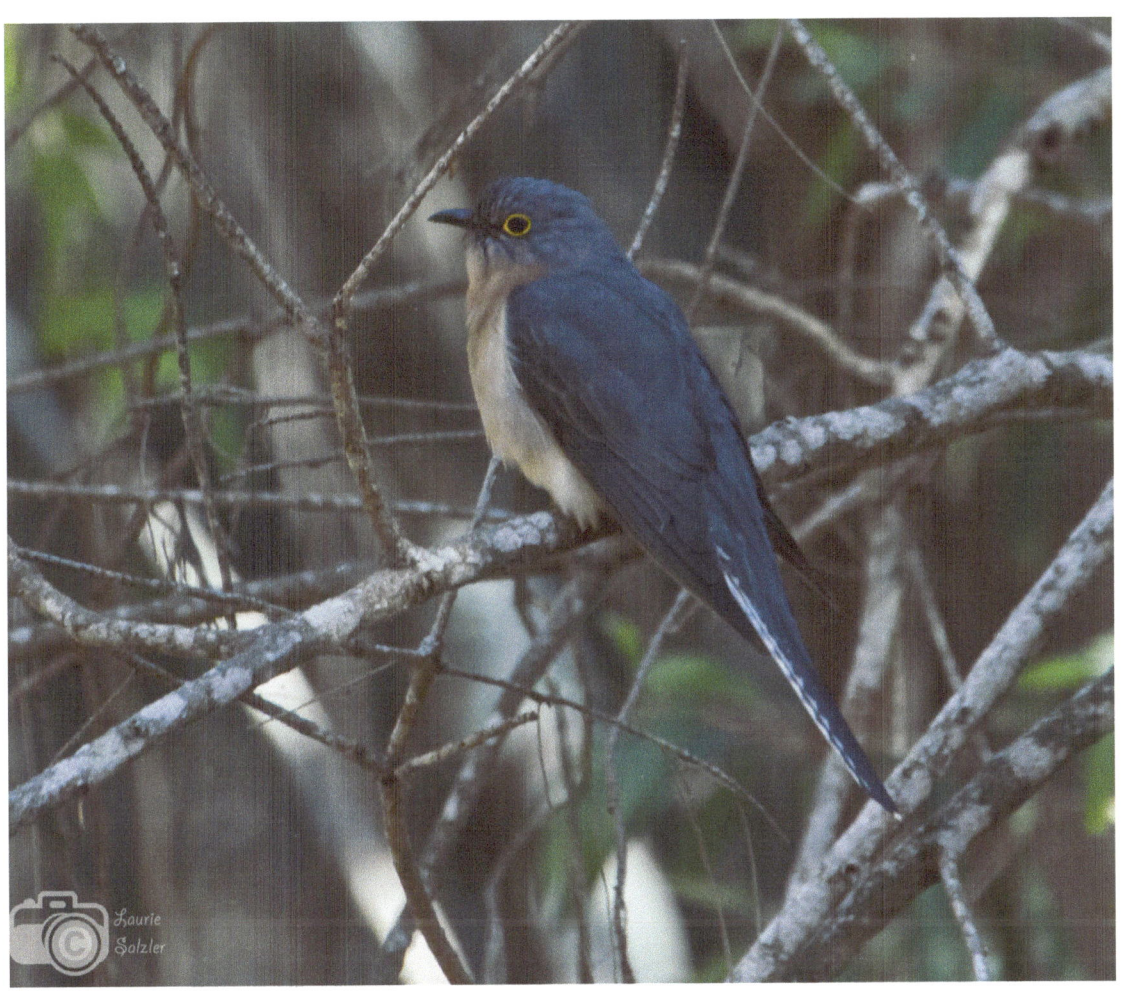

Fan-tailed Cuckoo
Ashby, NSW, Australia

Determination is forever the most aerodynamic shape and the best direct torpedoed conveyance.

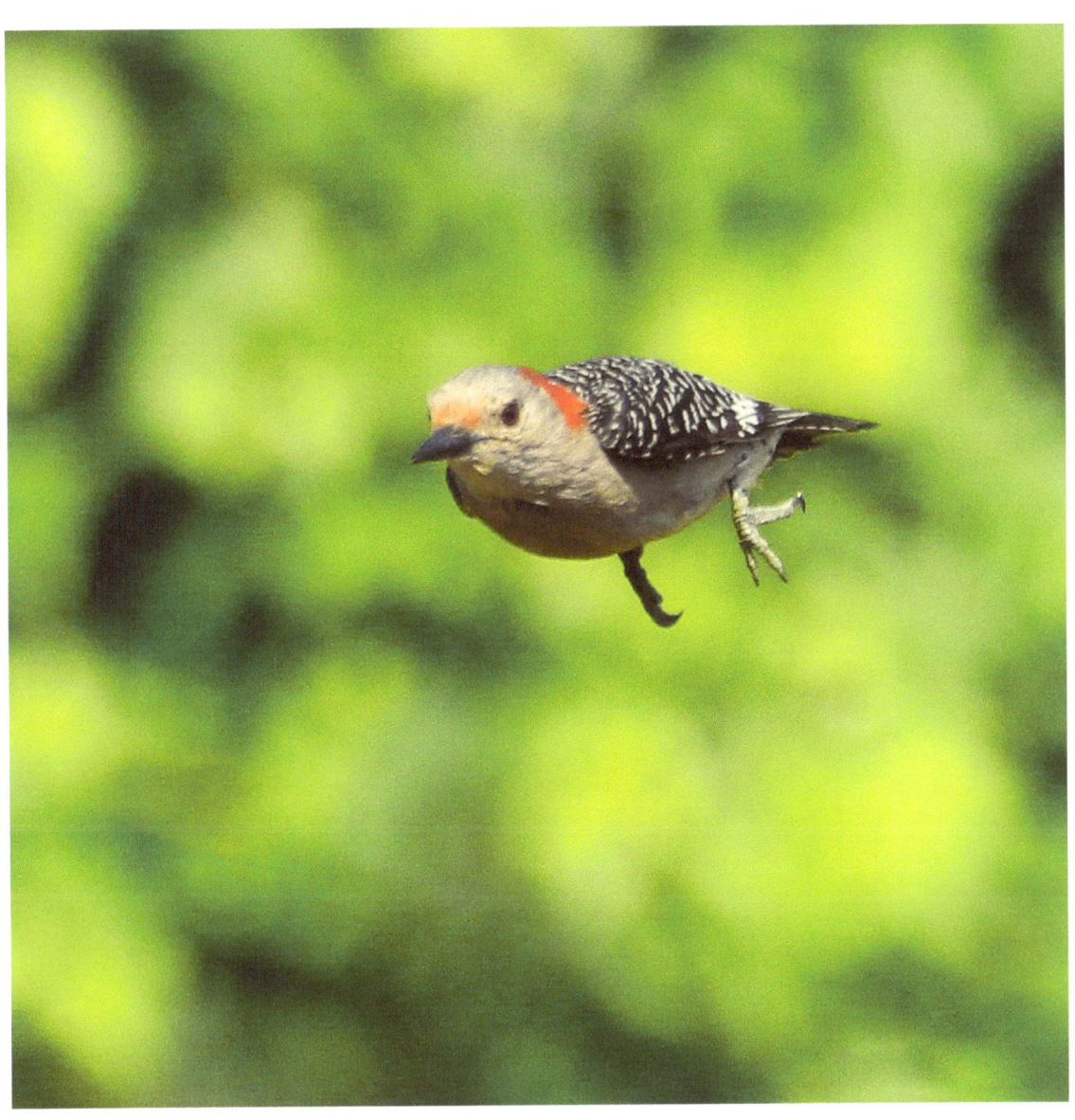

Red-bellied Woodpecker (Female)

*L*anding as gently as a sunbeam,

gathering life's fuel.

then flying away to the next garden,

the next welcoming blossom:

it is a life's work.

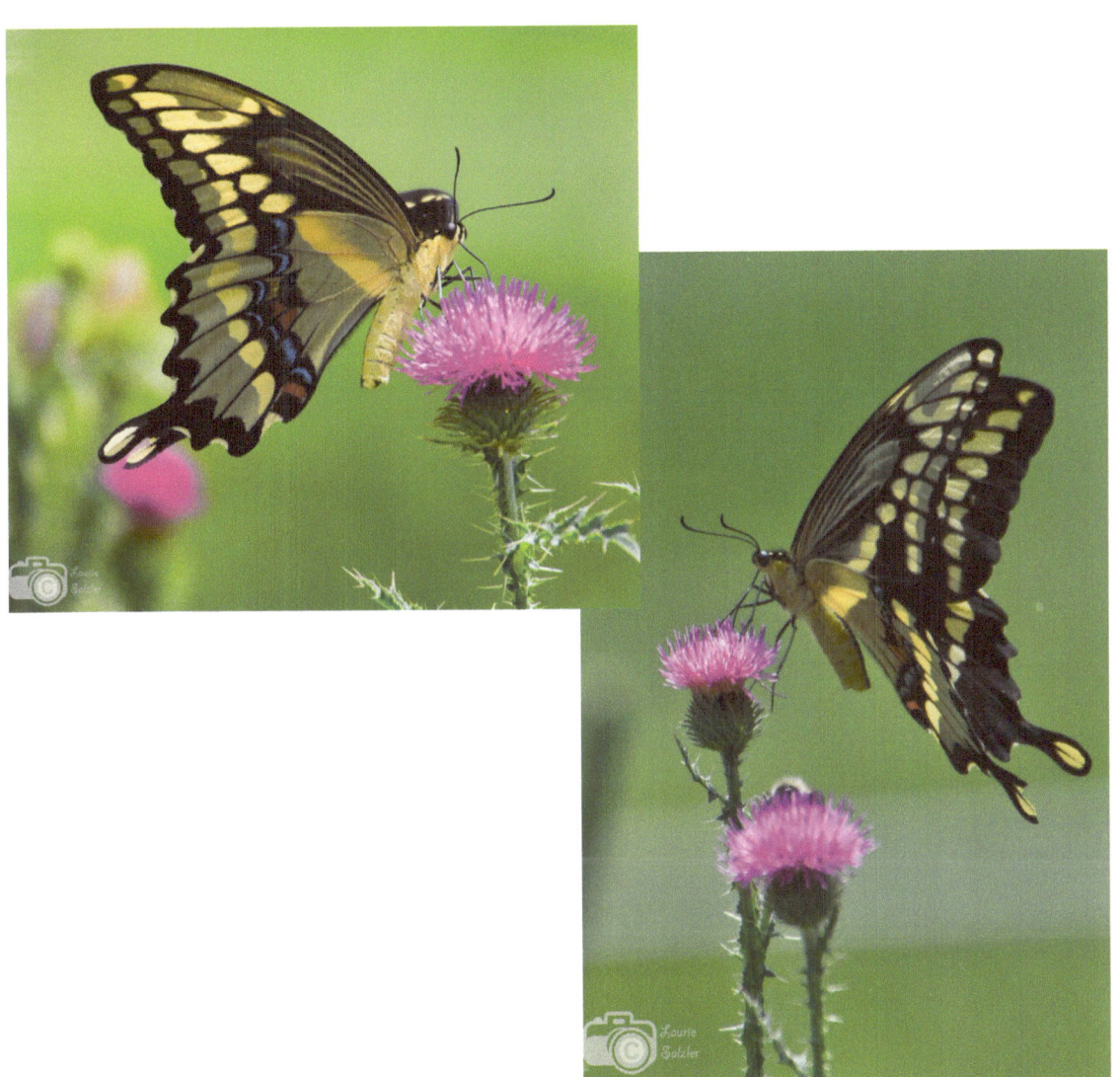

Giant Swallowtail
Ann Arbor, Michigan

Flexibility to attend to what itches,

to pay attention to the simple needs,

perhaps a strain but the results are satisfying.

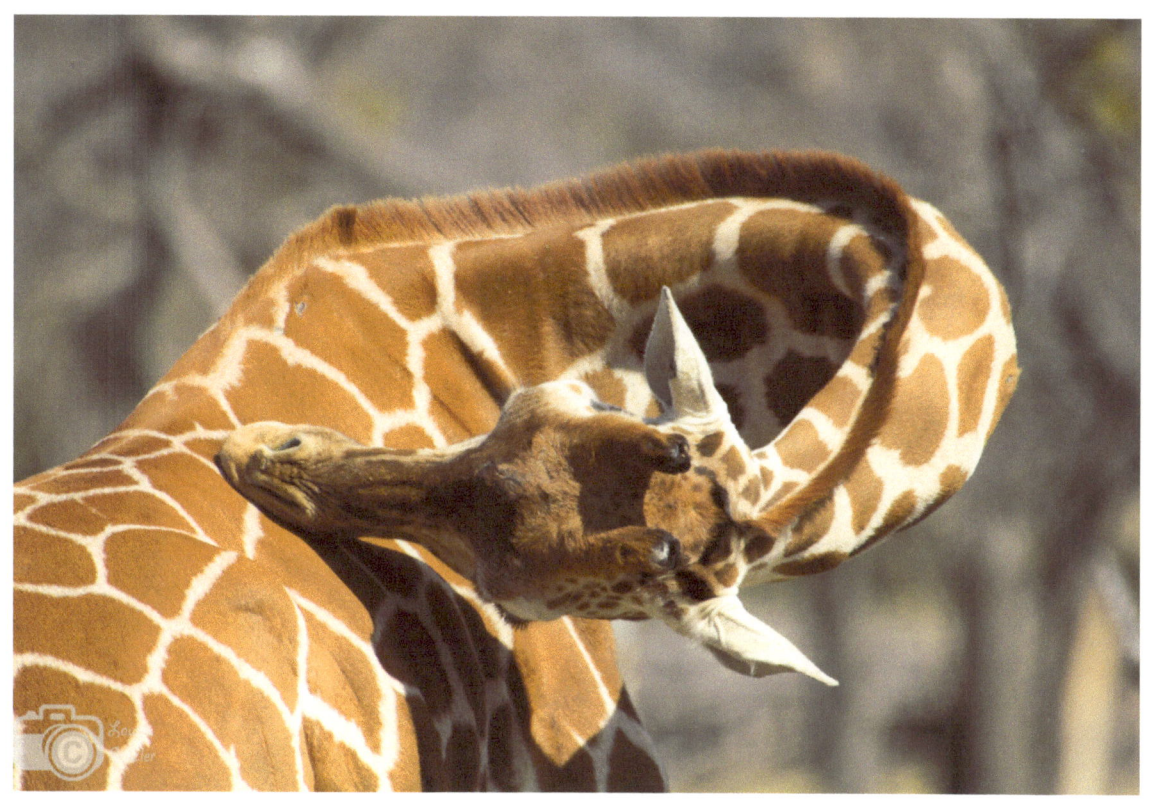

Giraffe
Fossil Rim, Texas

*Moving ahead with steady patience,
we can see what is just beyond,
nestled in the clouds over the next hill,
in the fallen away valley,
attending to progress—apace.*

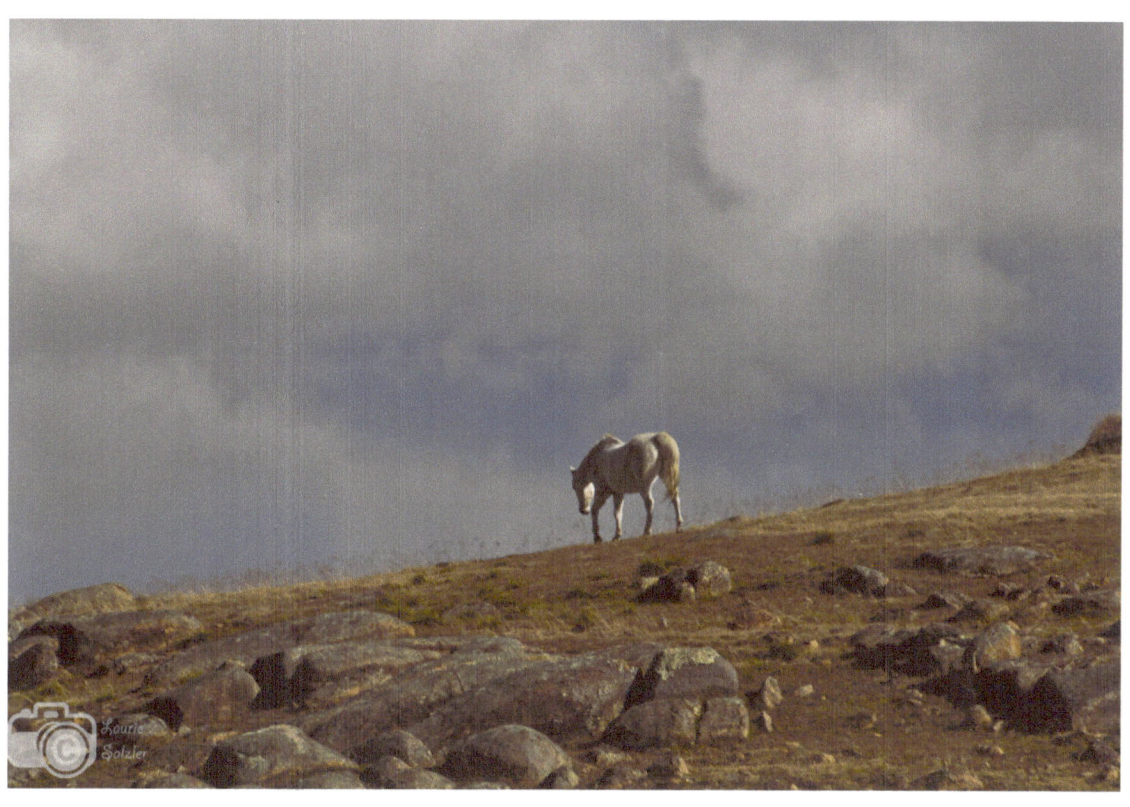

New South Wales, Australia

Wisping in the gentle breeze,
in the soft light, grasses accede to the push of air.
Fog swallows the sounds of the bookends
—daybreak, and evening.

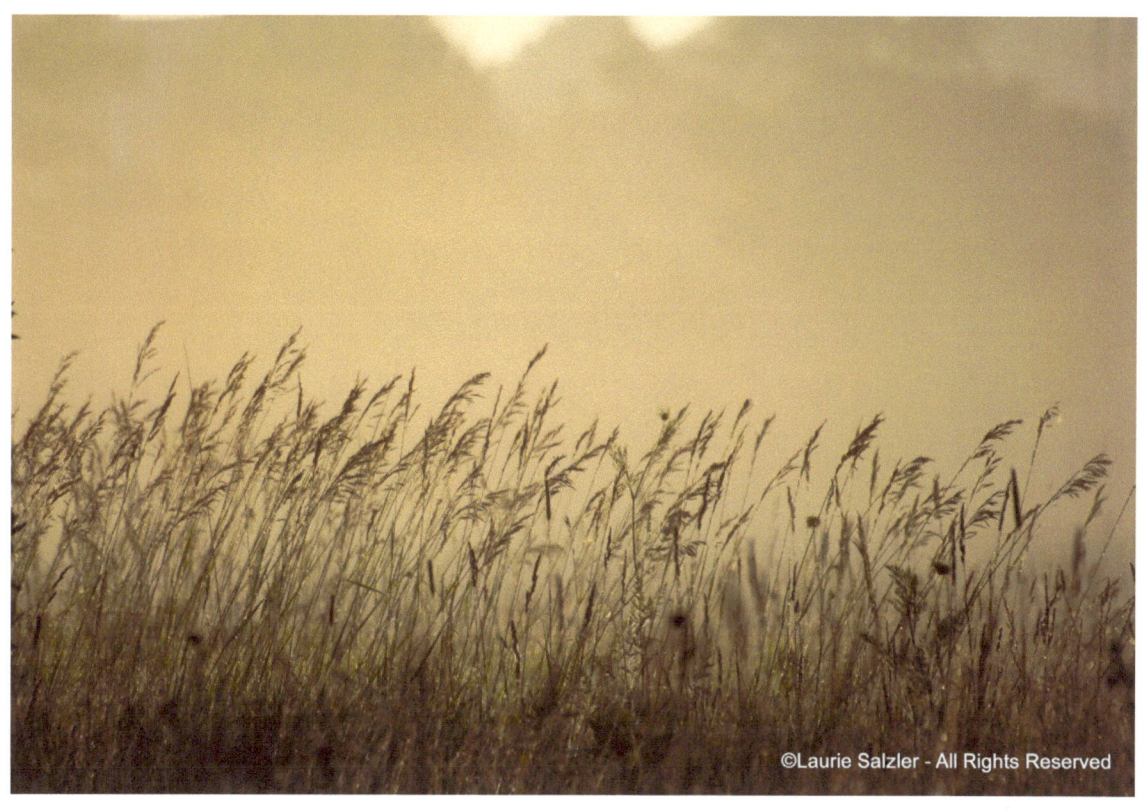

Ann Arbor, Michigan

Perched on the bend,

appreciating the view,

there is a time for gathering energy and perseverance.

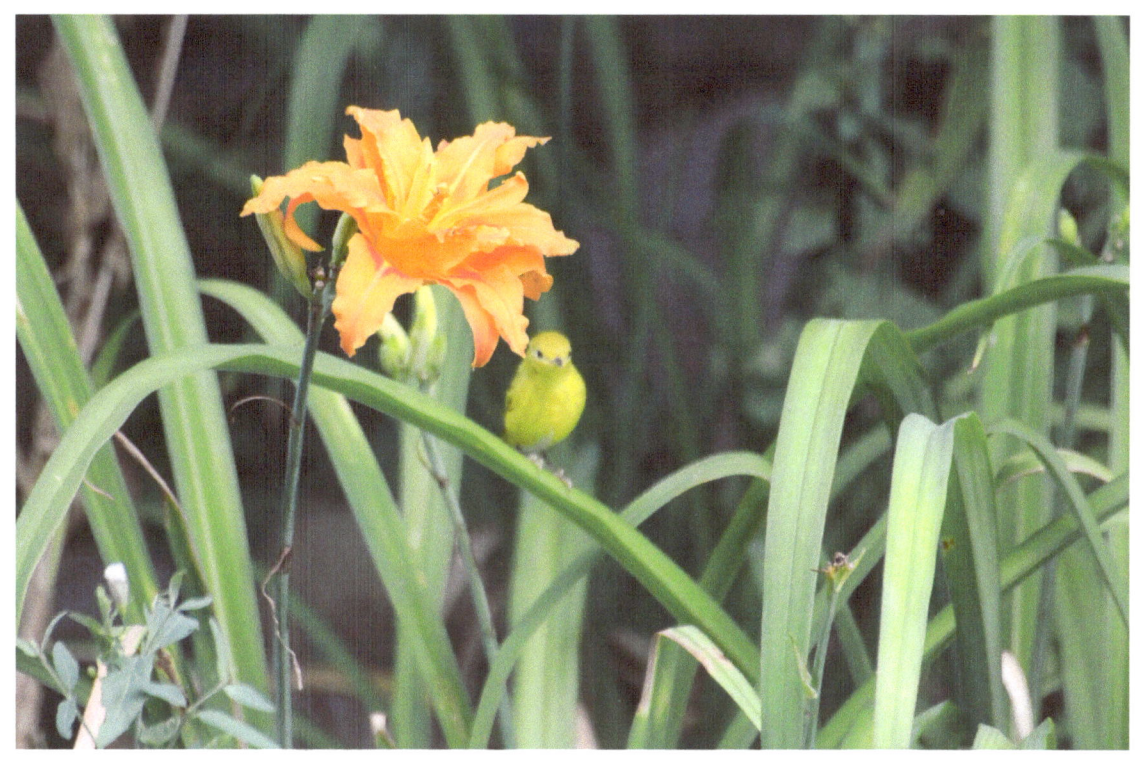

Lily & Yellow Warbler
Ann Arbor, Michigan

*The prickly thistle,
with its difficult and challenging abrasiveness,
offers necessary sustenance and mooring.*

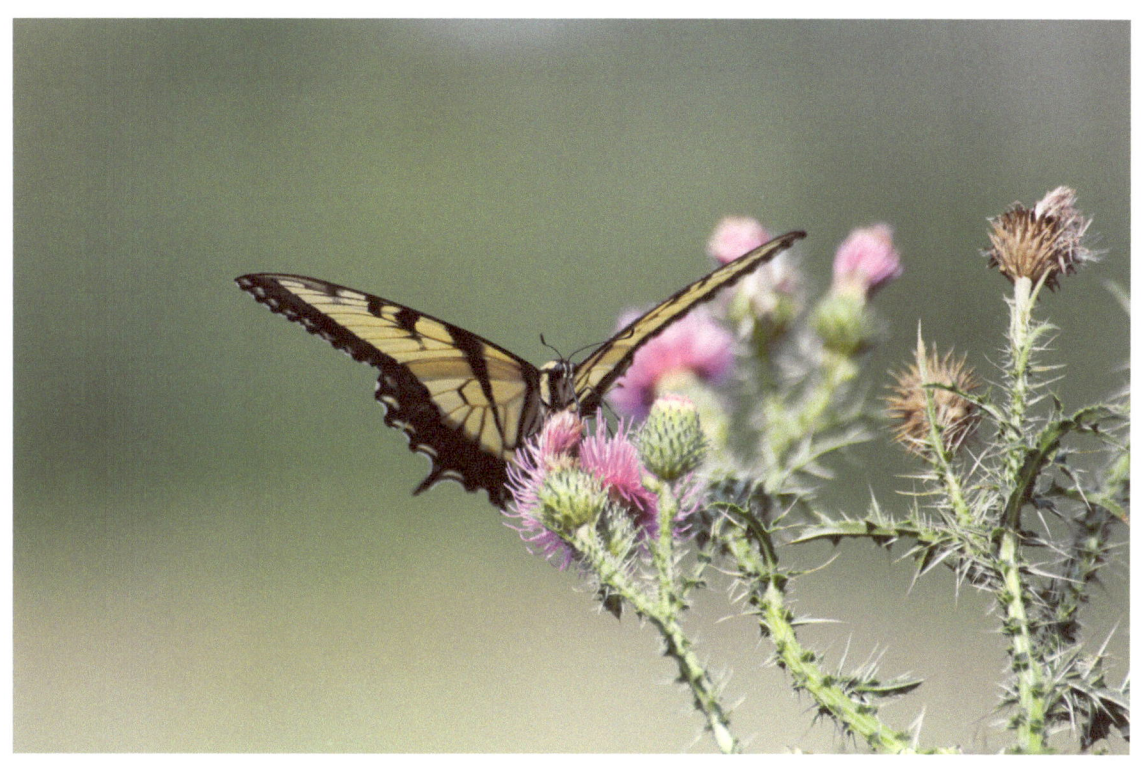

Giant Swallowtail
Ann Arbor, Michigan

From a different perspective,

from the unusual view,

there is often extraordinary magnificence.

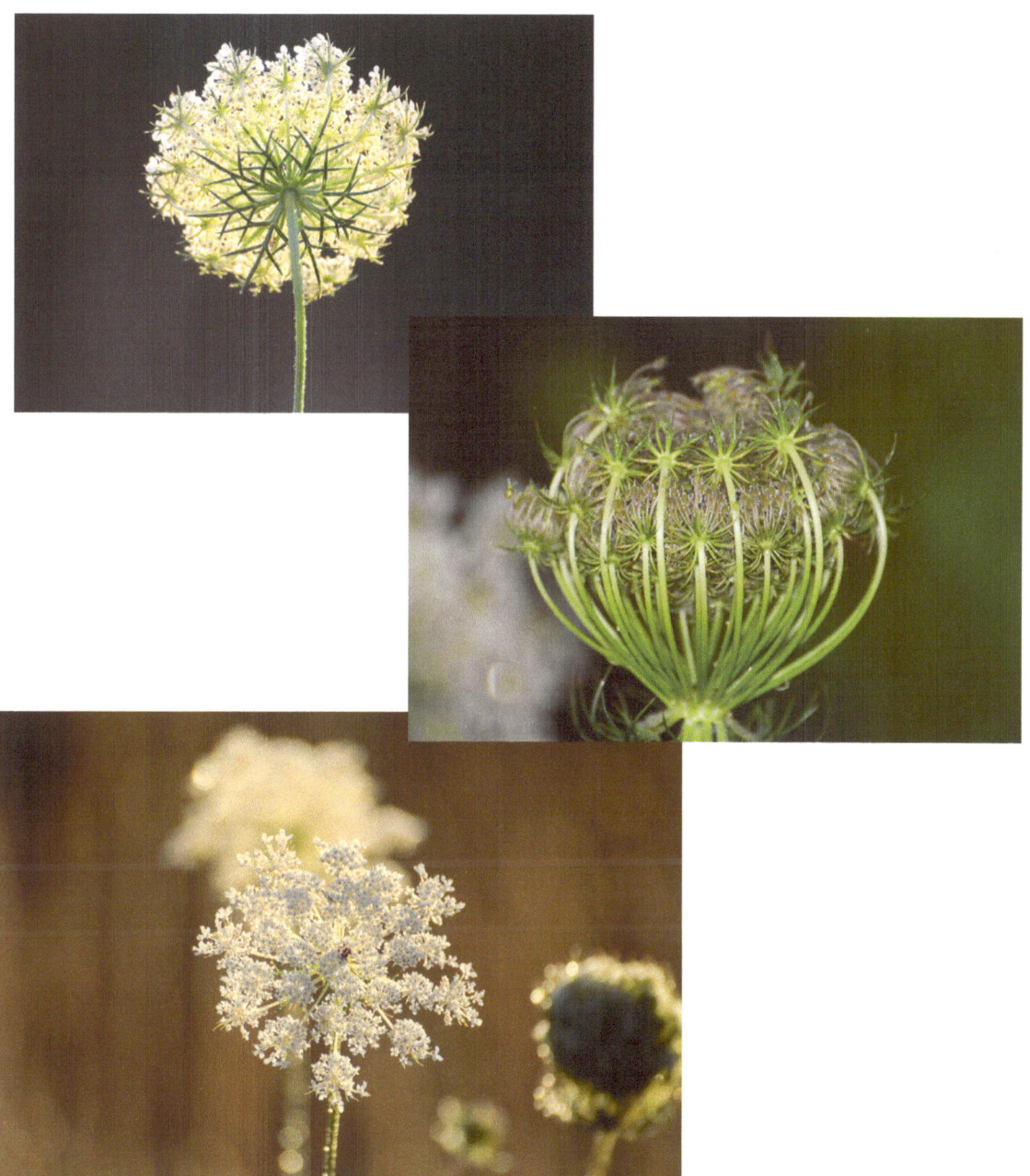

Queen Anne's Lace
Ann Arbor, Michigan

Plenty to share,
nature feeds the composite hunger.

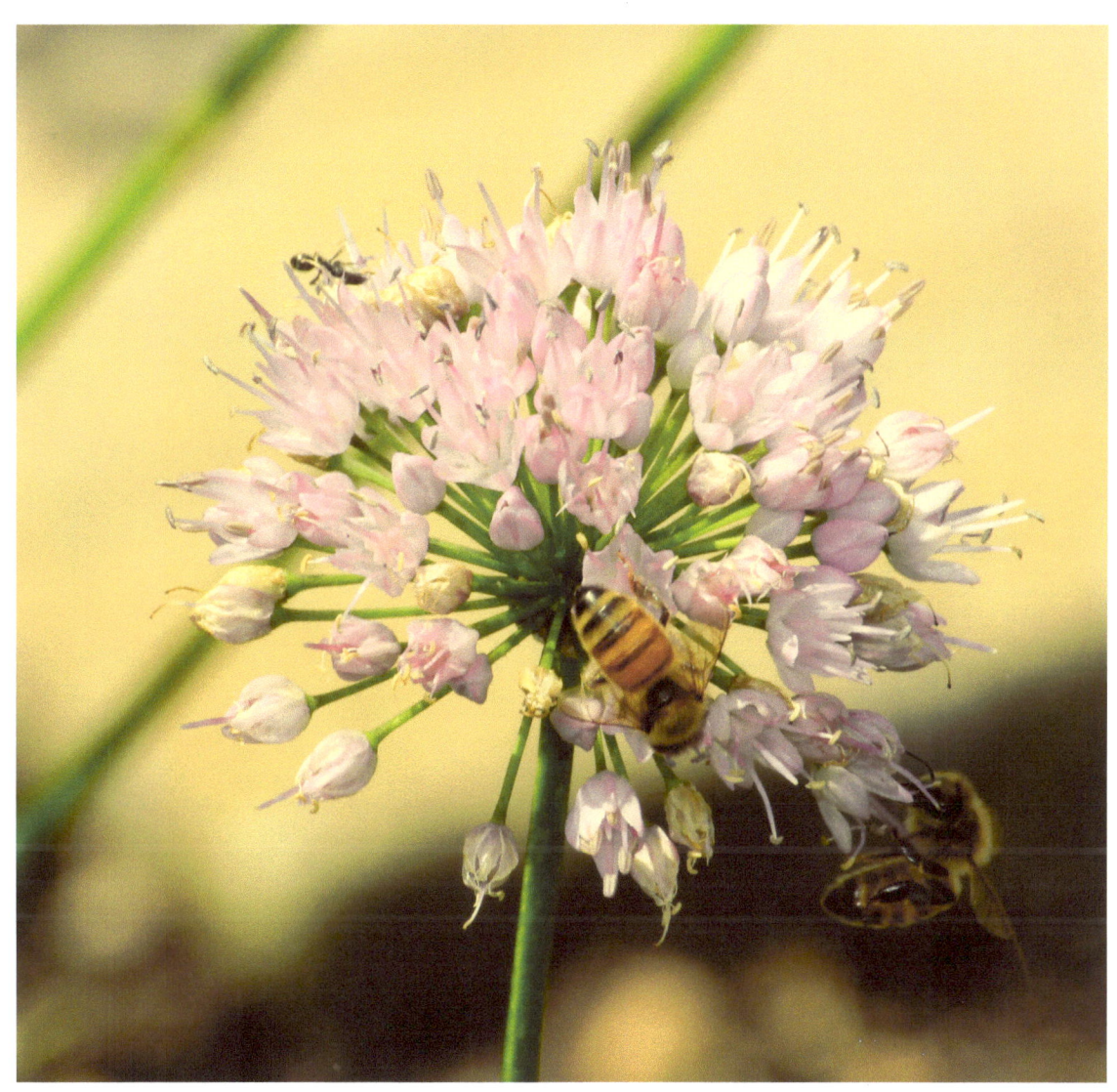

Ann Arbor, Michigan

Sometimes the most significance comes from the arch of necessity, the curve of perpetuation—connections of ongoing life.

Eye of the Beholder 63

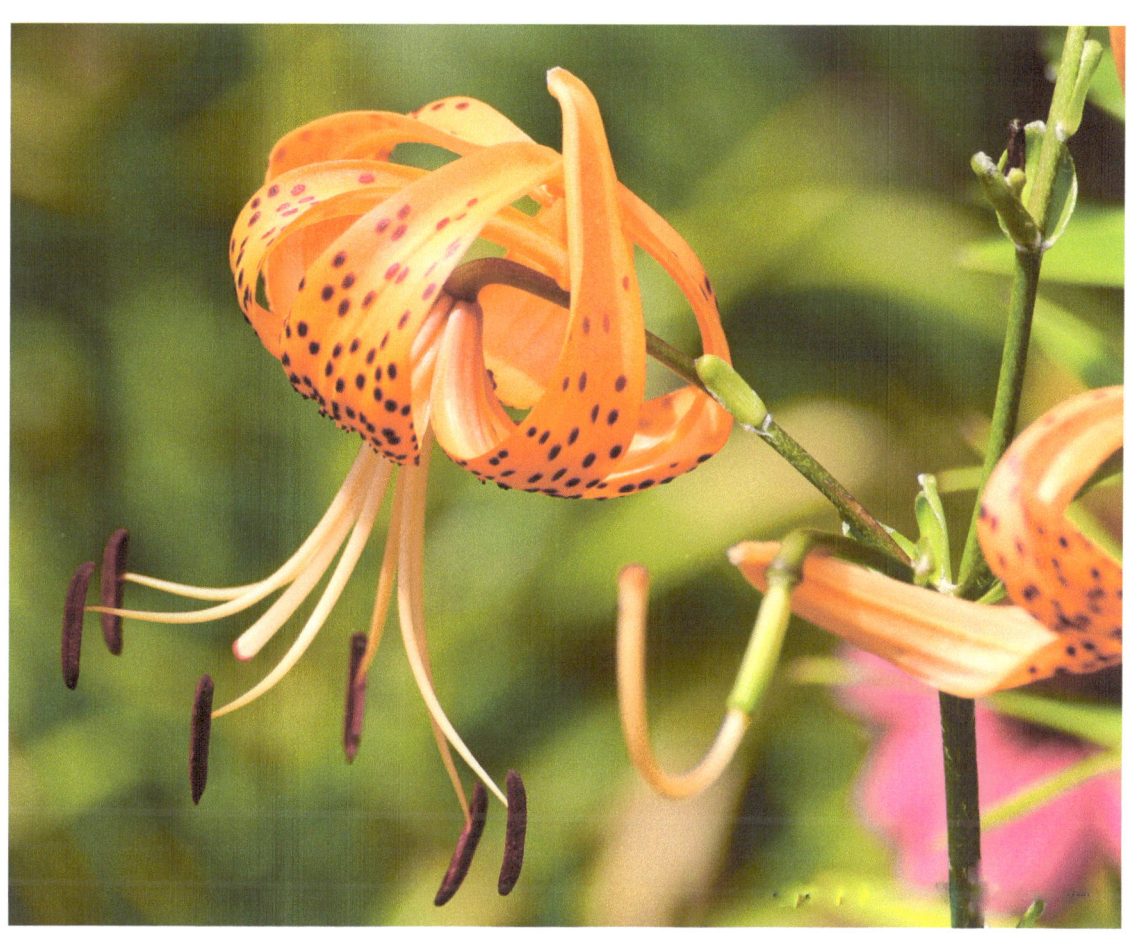

Ann Arbor, Michigan

*J*ust before,

just as the light shows and tints the day,

the tall branches hold the welcome,

offer the roost of beginning.

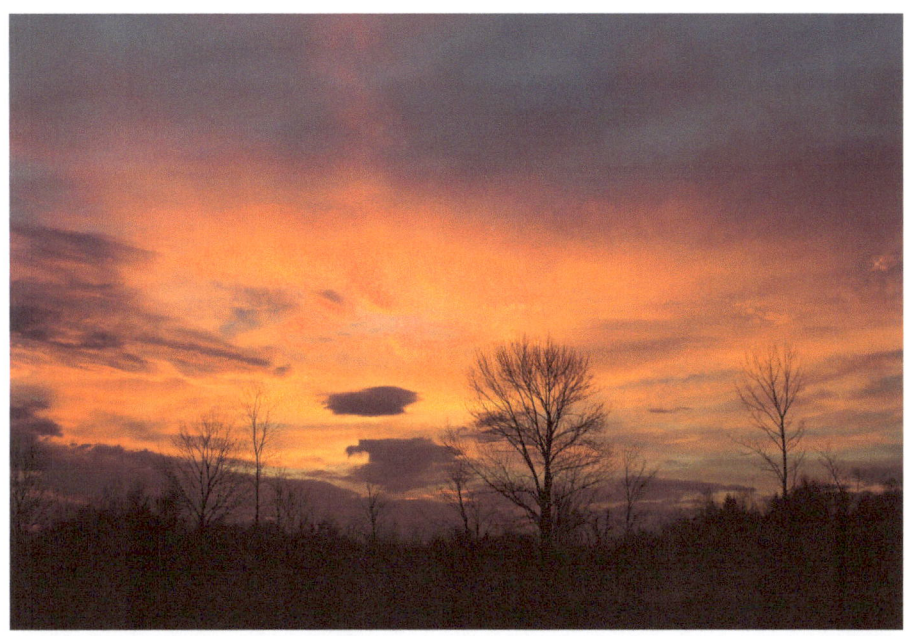

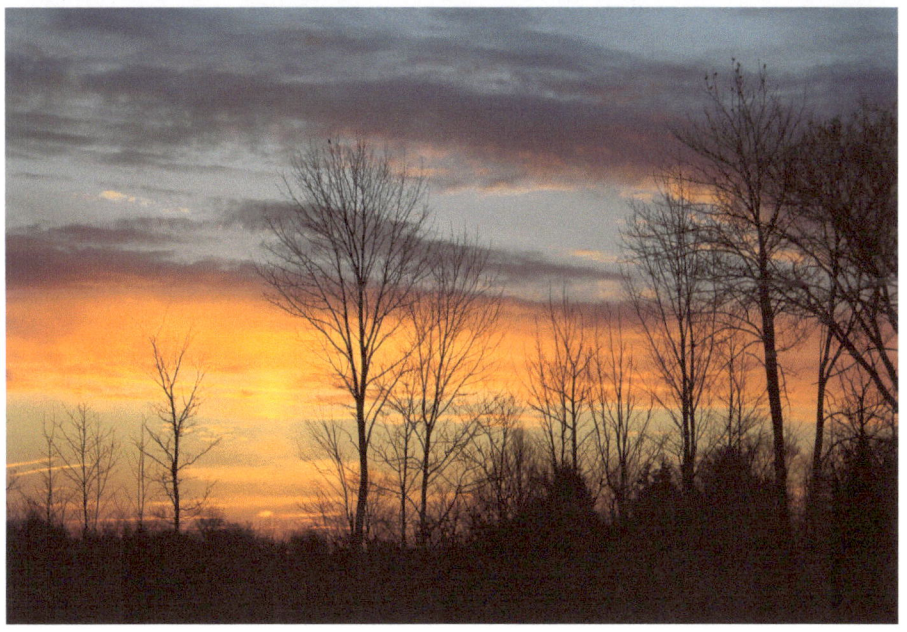

Derby, New York

Delicate symmetry in balance as in color,

reflecting and protecting,

unique patterns of complexity.

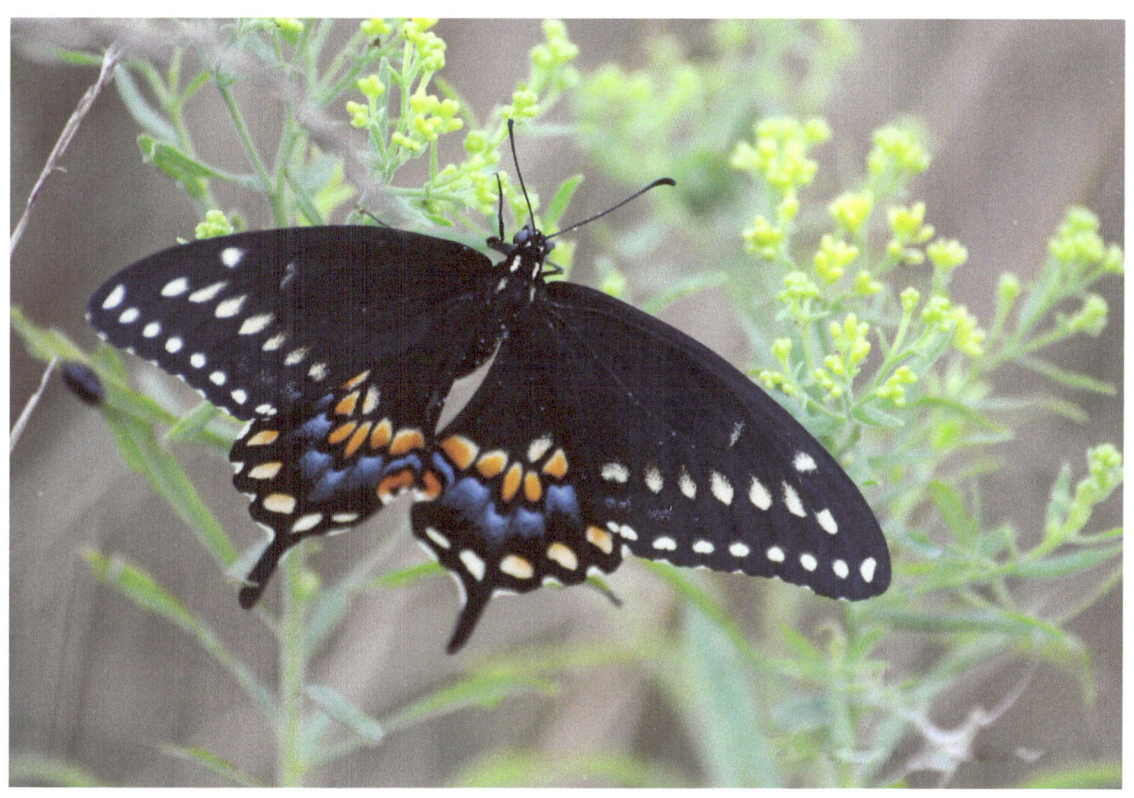

Black Swallowtail
Ann Arbor, Michigan

*There is a moment when the calculations
and plan decidedly succeed
in perfect homecomings.*

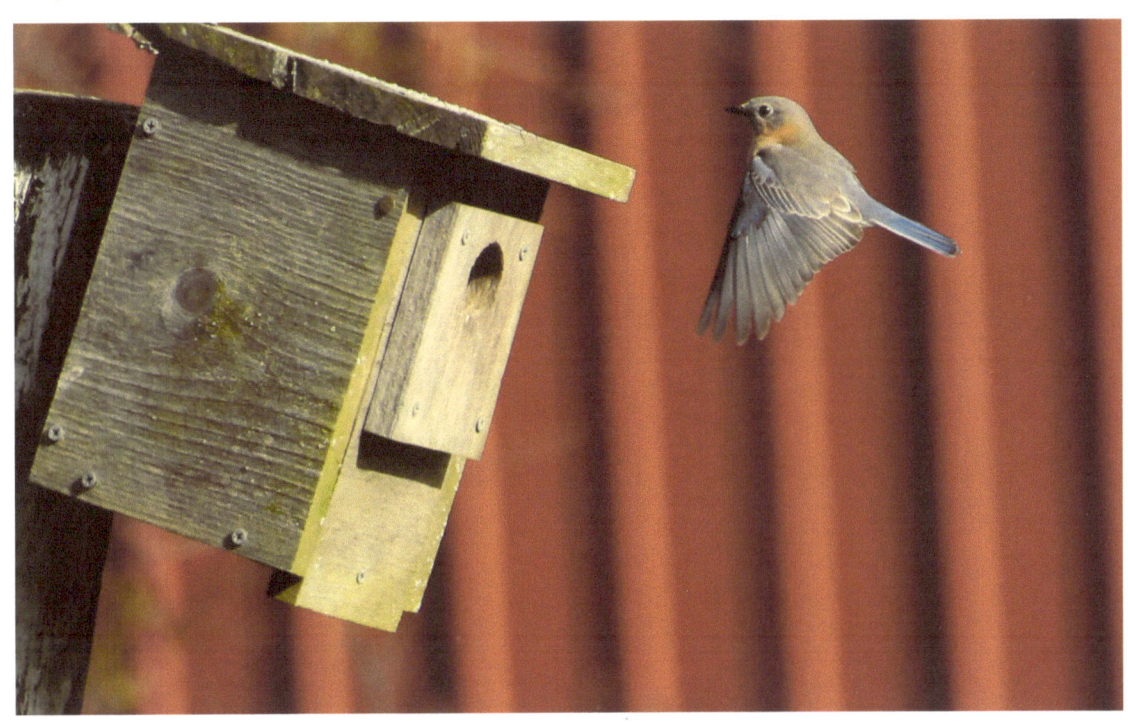

Eastern Bluebird

Derby, New York

Shouting and vibrant,

the flower is never abashed to bring joyful sunbeams,

shining in every corner.

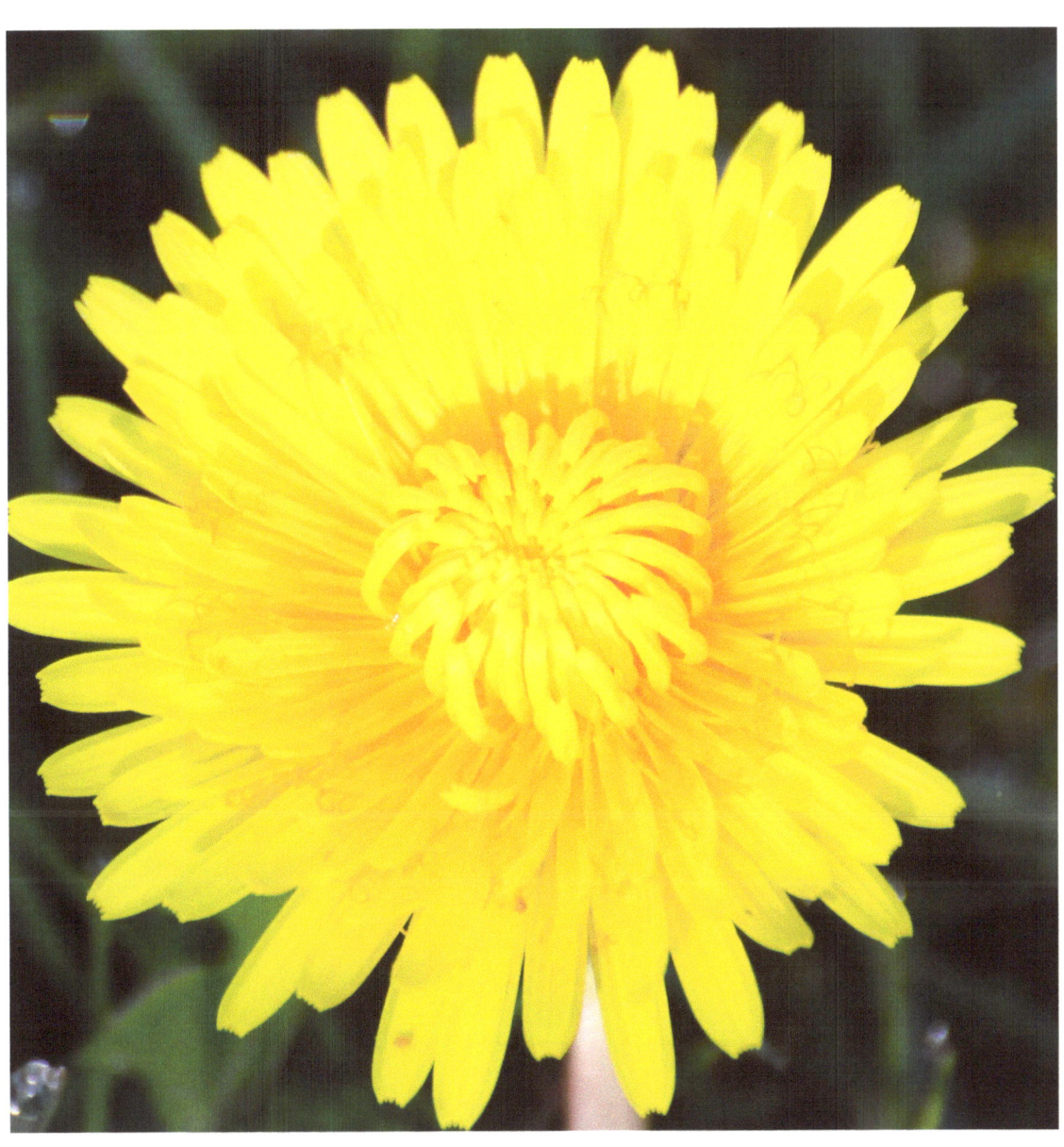

Never a weed
but rather a feathered blossom,
the dandelion captures dew in preparation to spread,
the iridescent drops cling and mirror,
drops focus the work of light.

Eye of the Beholder 73

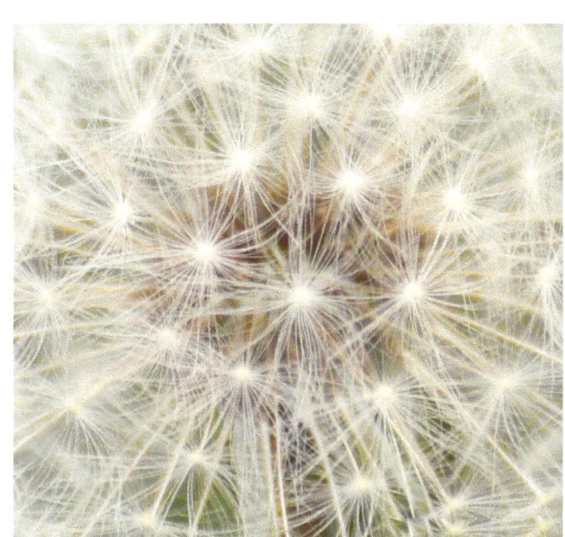
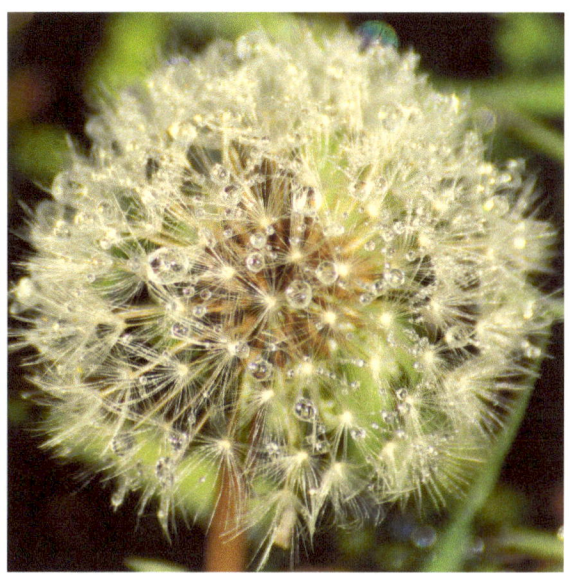
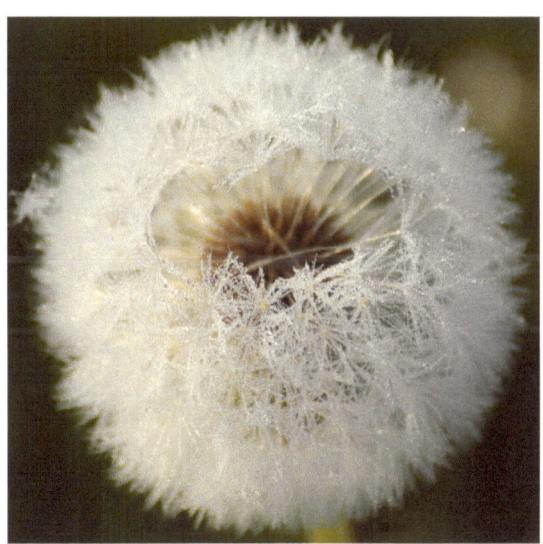
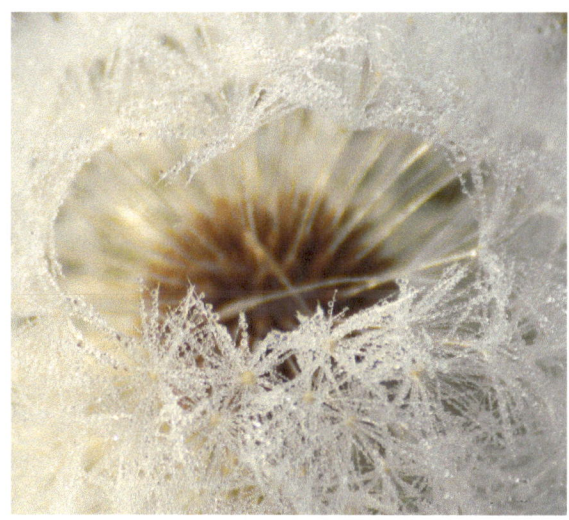

Dandelion

*Holding on to the droplets
and valuing the plentiful gifts of nature,
beauty sustains.*

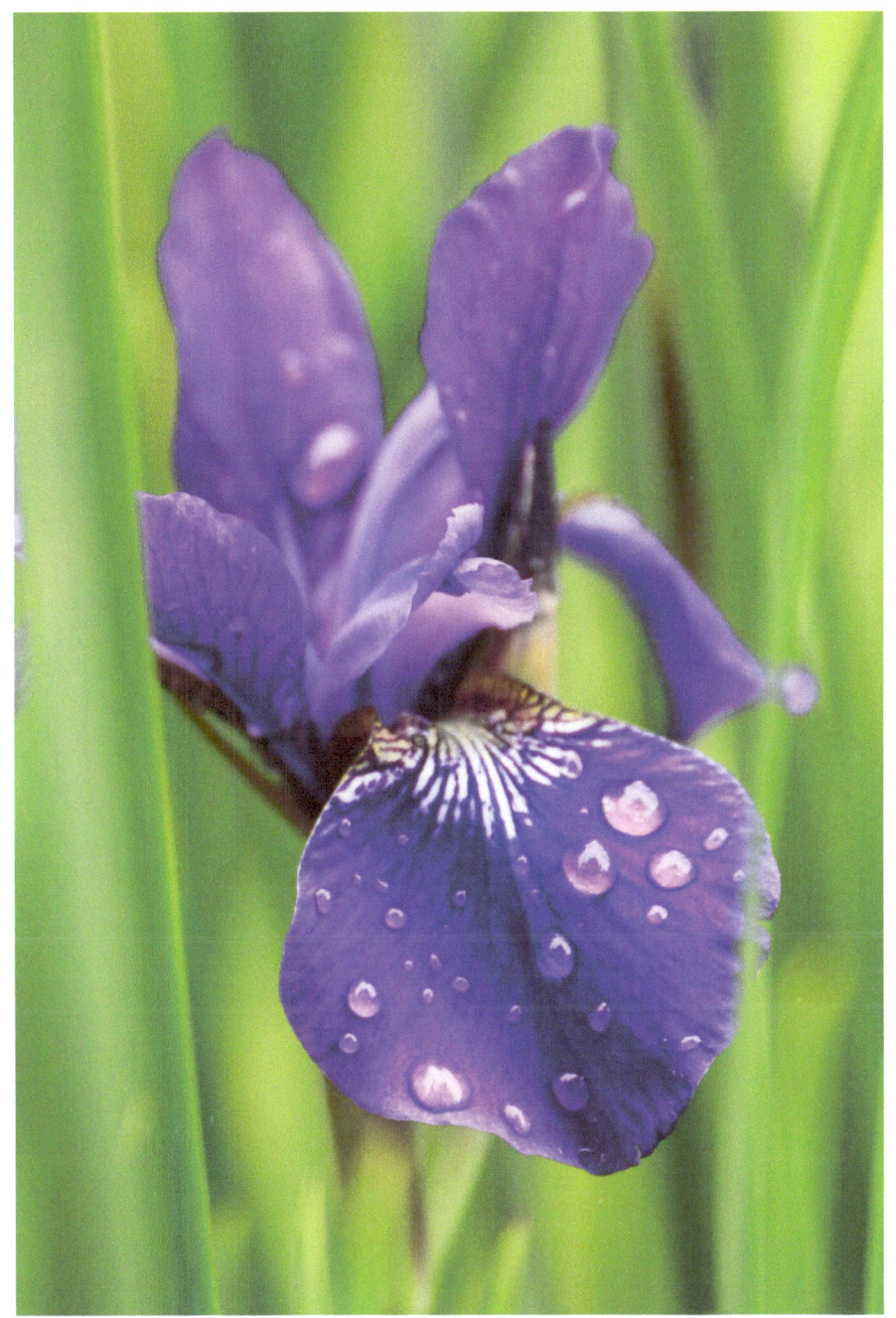

Iris

Iridescence
and an instantaneous capture—
diminutive and also profound.

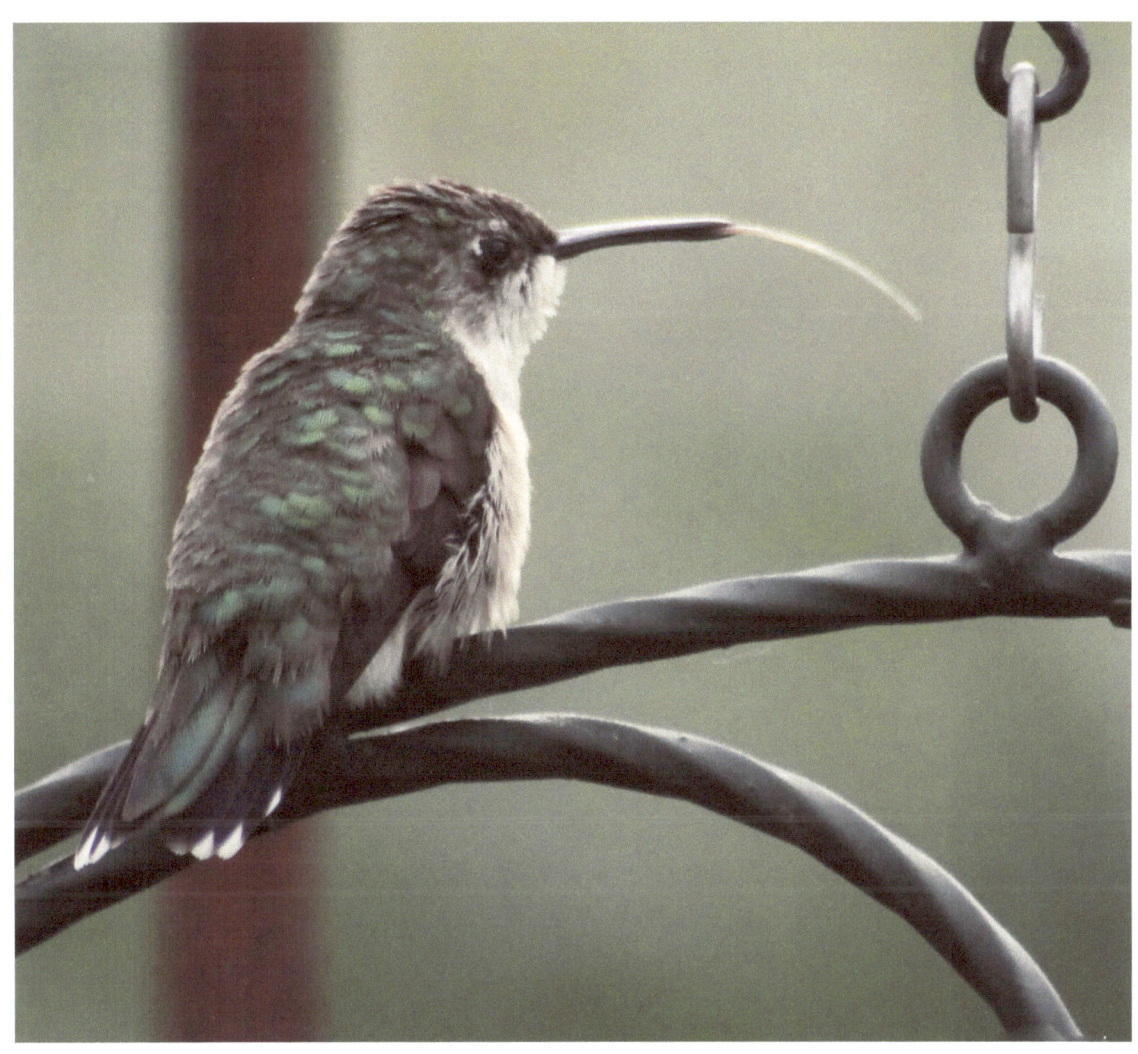

Ruby-throated Hummingbird (female)
Ann Arbor, Michigan

Backlit with sun,

the whispering shapes stand in calm agreement,

in a harmony of quiet still meadow.

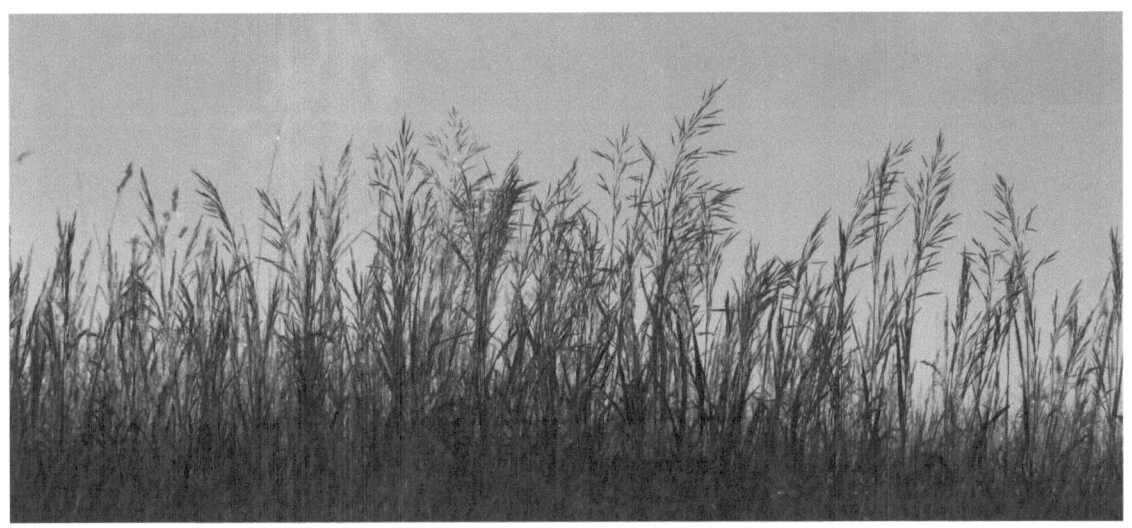

In the family of things,

there are caring communications taught and learned.

In the moments of awareness,

time must be taken to attend to the young,

to the bonding and necessities.

There will always be a cautious heightened alertness,

but time to "be" together is as important as the recognition

of potential dangers,

and for us, appreciation without invasion.

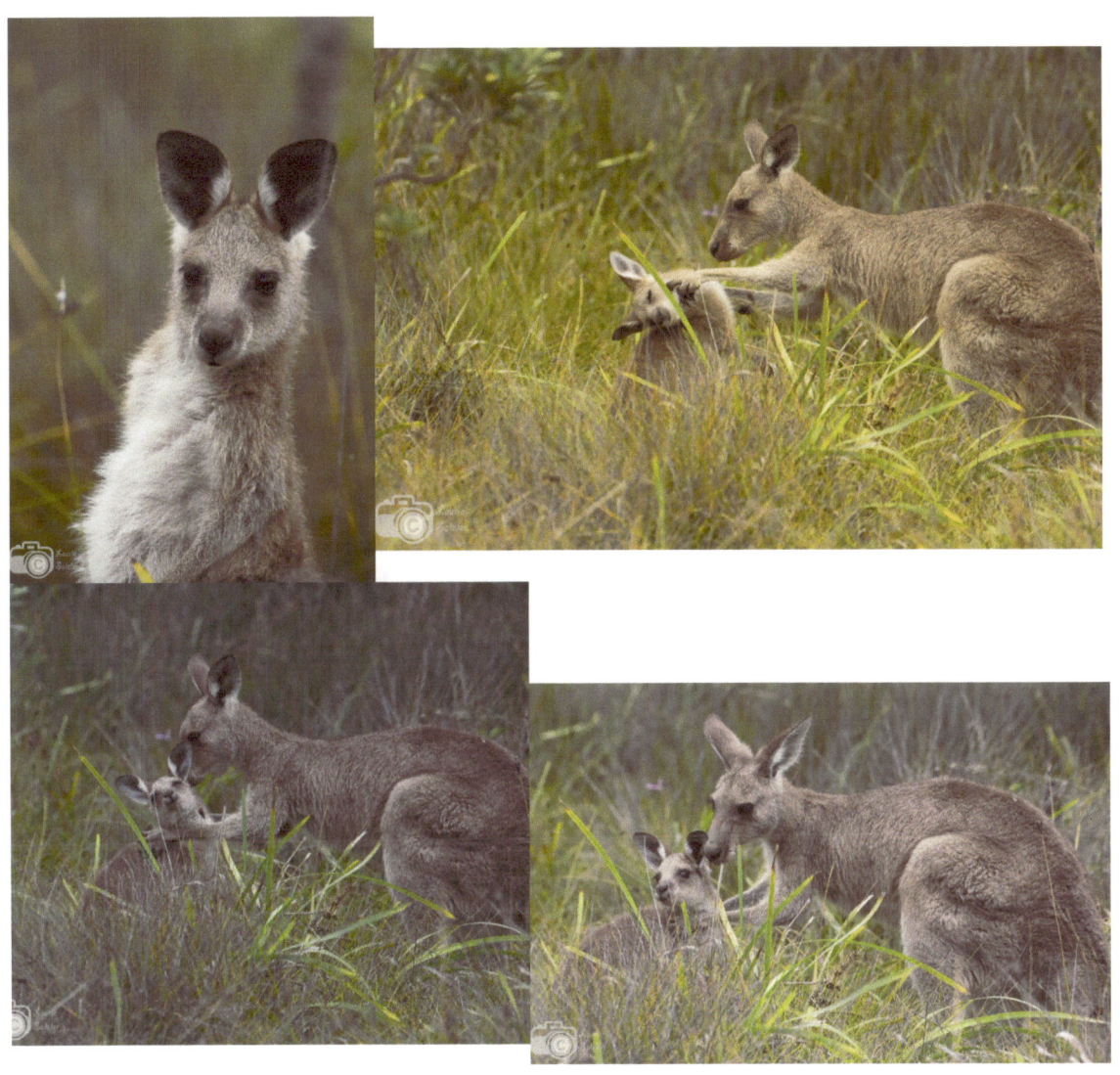

Eastern Grey Kangaroo
NSW, Australia

Thoughtfully quiet and quietly thoughtful—

sweet moment captured of a Joey,

just a contemplative Joey.

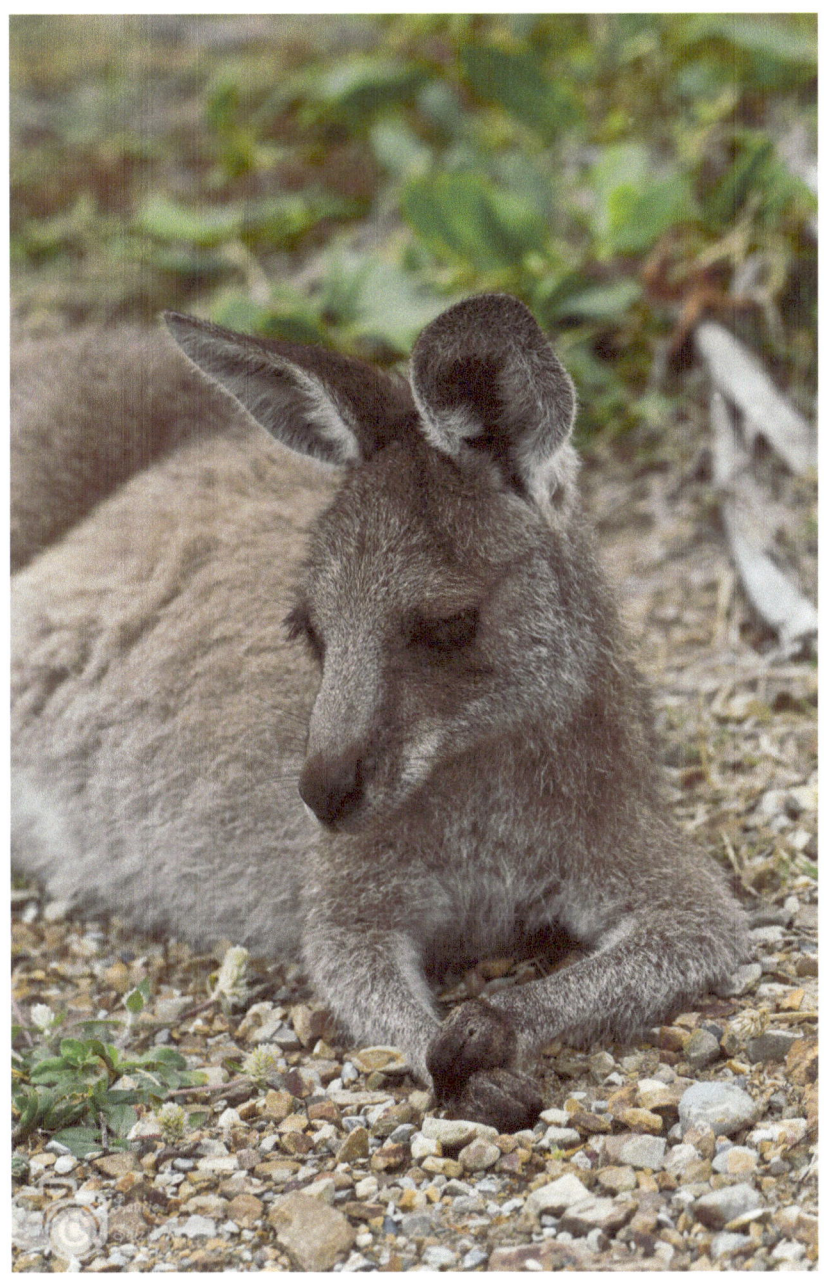

Eastern Grey Kangaroo
Brooms Head, NSW, Australia

Inquisitive and appreciating a stop for a drink, thankful for the offering.

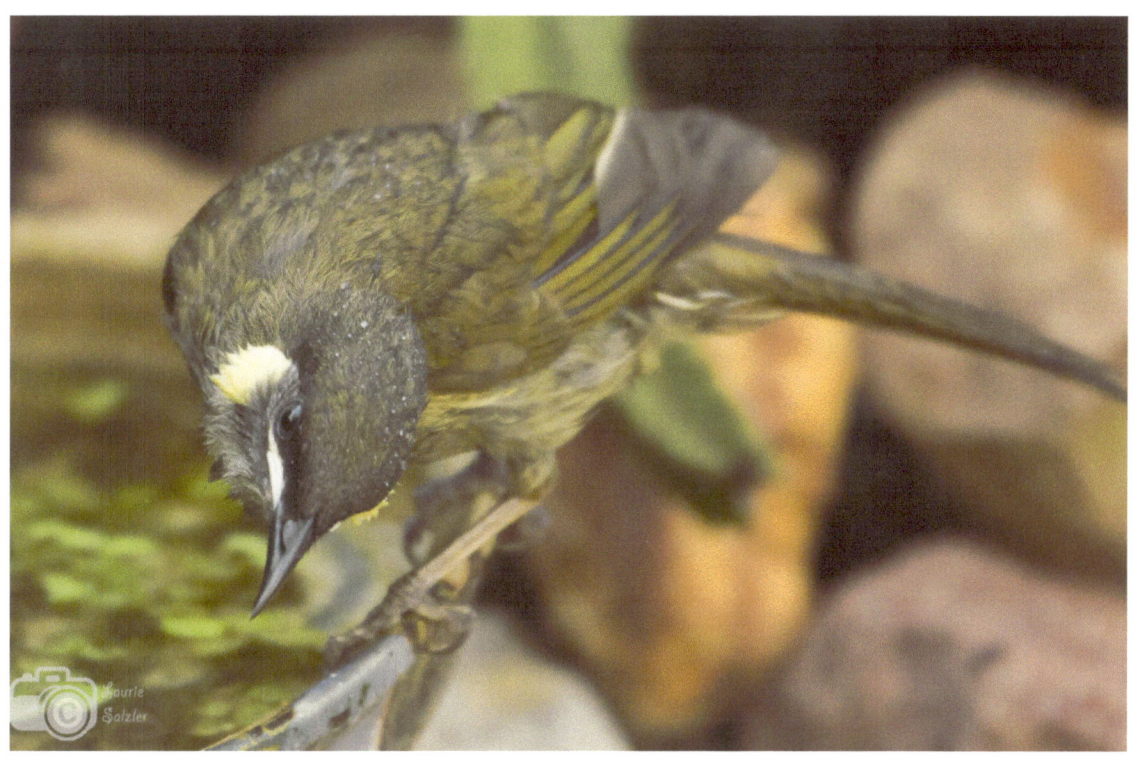

Lewin's Honeyeater
Ashby, NSW, Australia

*Moments of use and re-use,
best to adapt to change as needed
and receive the new definition.*

Eye of the Beholder 87

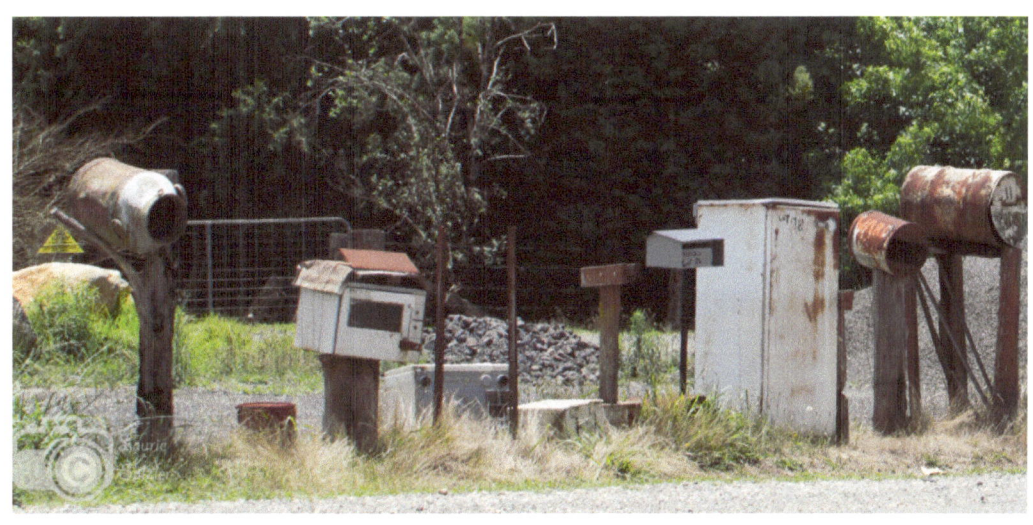

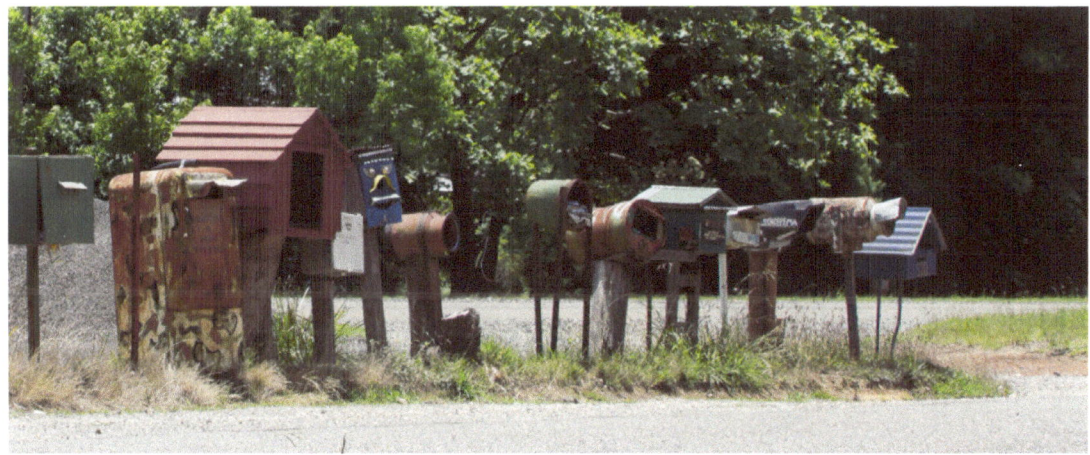

NSW, Australia

*Wonderful rewards are offered when vigilant watching,
and being aware of what might pass by is keenly practiced.
Keeping soft eyes and an open expectancy,
the best opportunities present.*

Red Fox

Derby, New York

Flitting among the flowers,

seeking where to momentarily settle,

Monarch follows the light to a nimble landing.

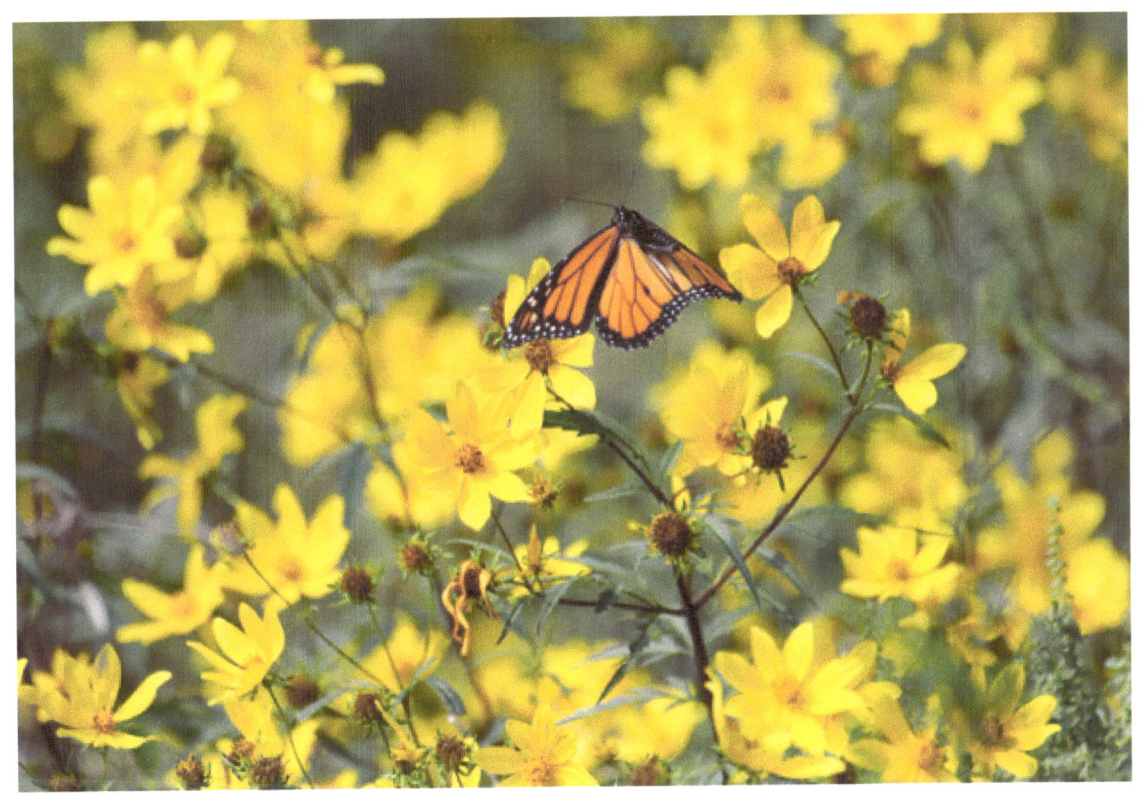

Monarch Butterfly

Derby, New York

Hidden in highlights of dew,
the individual beauty of each stalk,
the feathered tops of every blade,
blend to a wonder-filled softly undulating field.

Eye of the Beholder 93

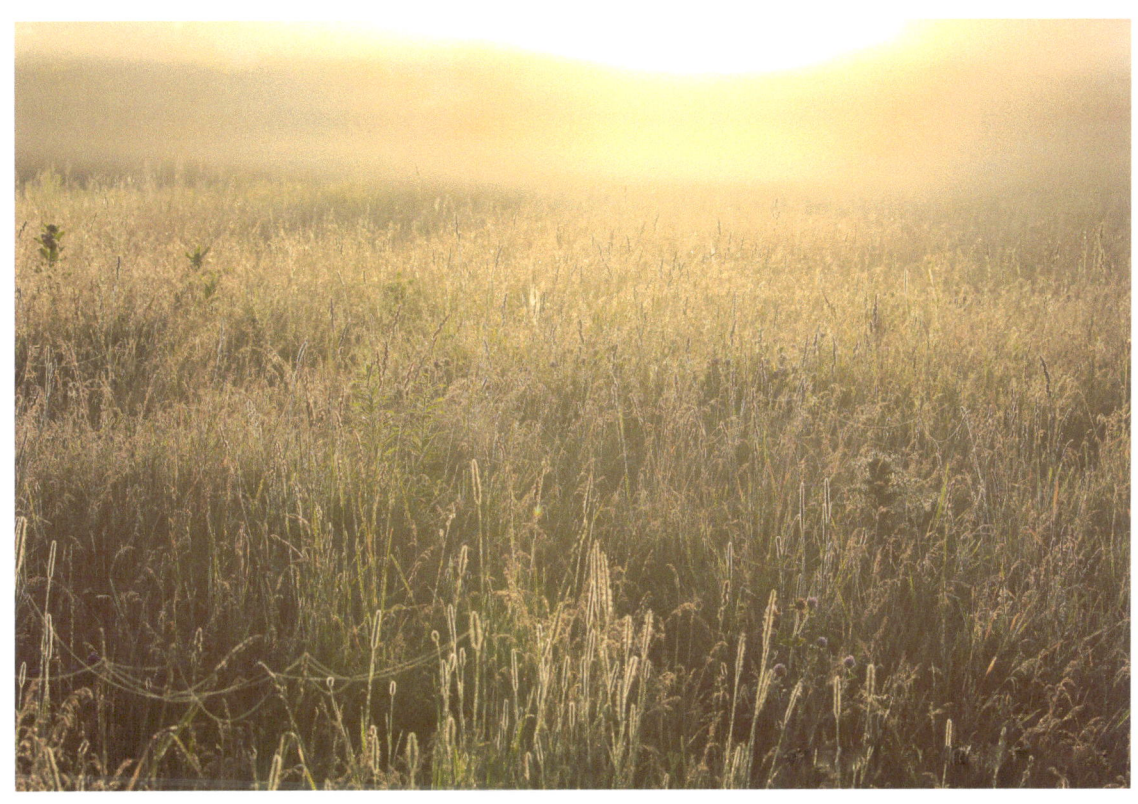

Ann Arbor, Michigan

Golden orange petals blaze the drops in shadow and glory.

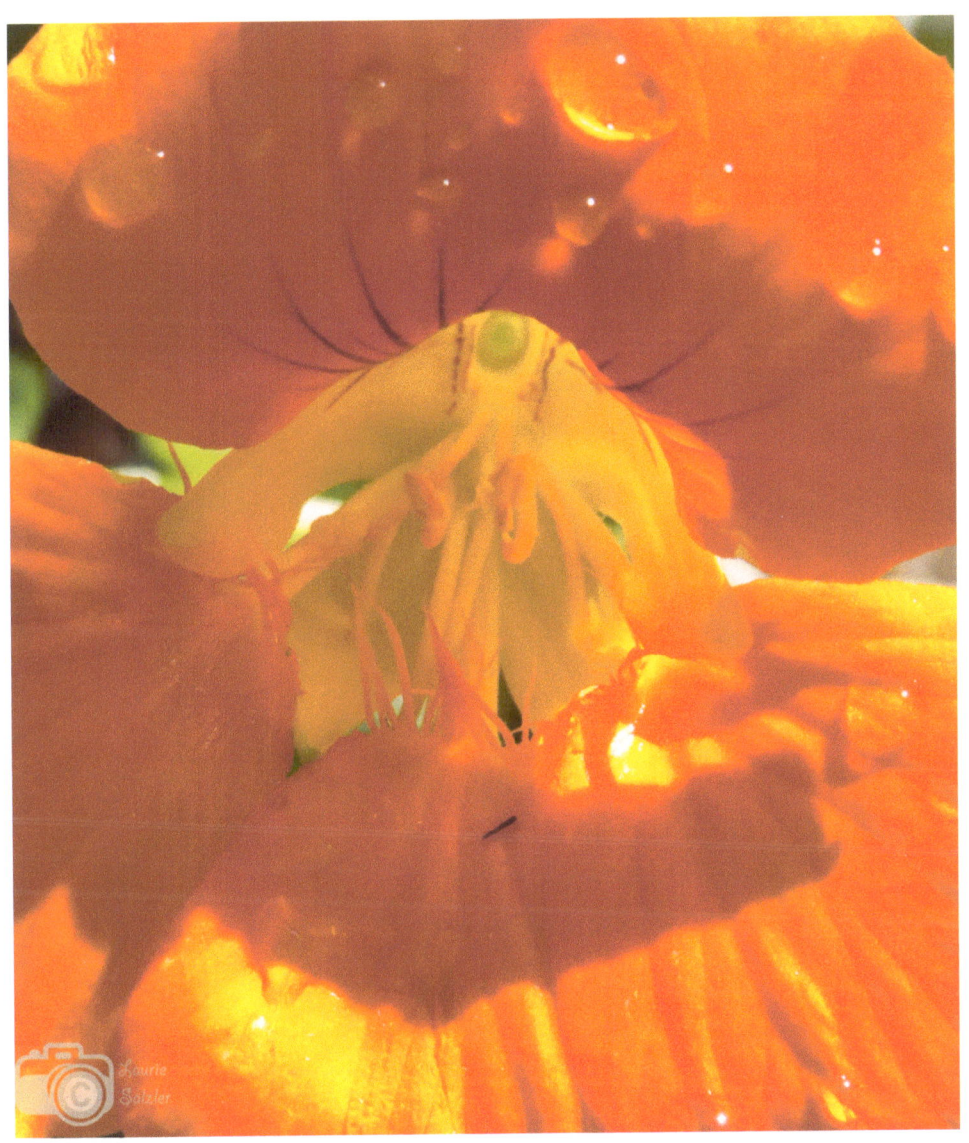

Nasturtium

Following usefulness,

after the last plug is sparked,

the parts salvaged and claimed for next,

rust and vegetation take the place of dirt road dust and hot pavement.

The truck is pastured.

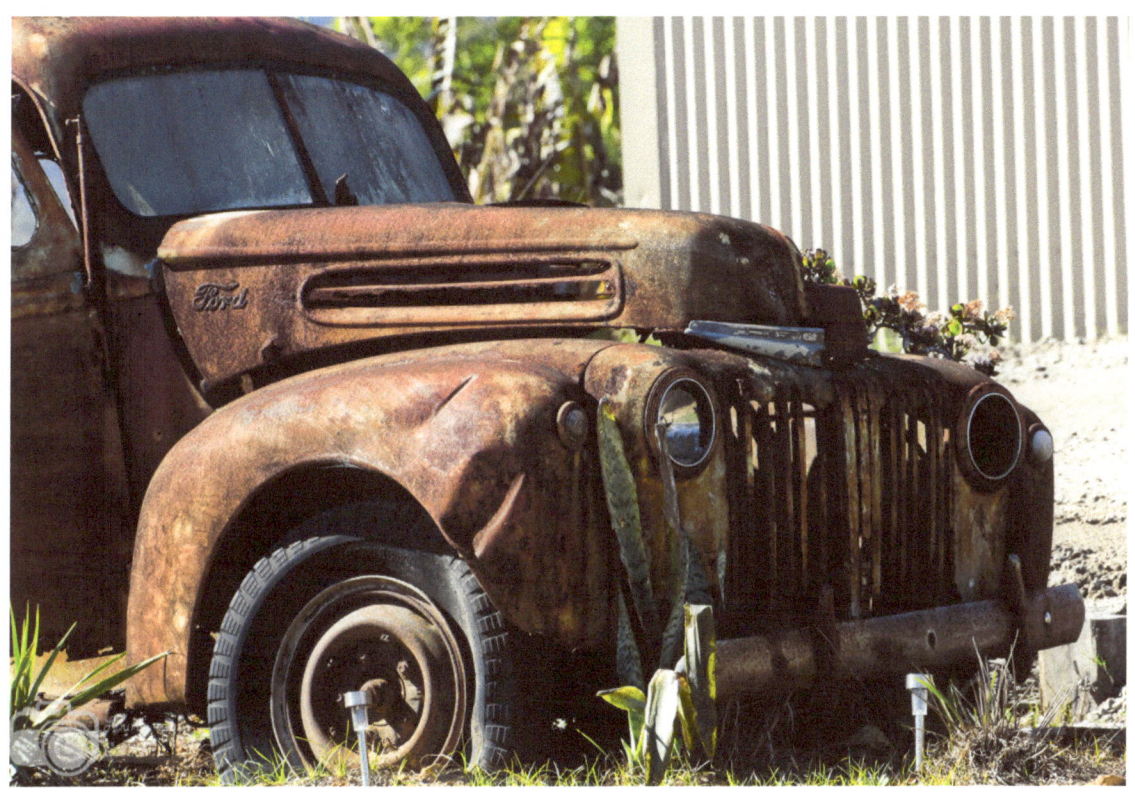

NSW, Australia

Inscrutable pole-sitter,
avian omniscience.

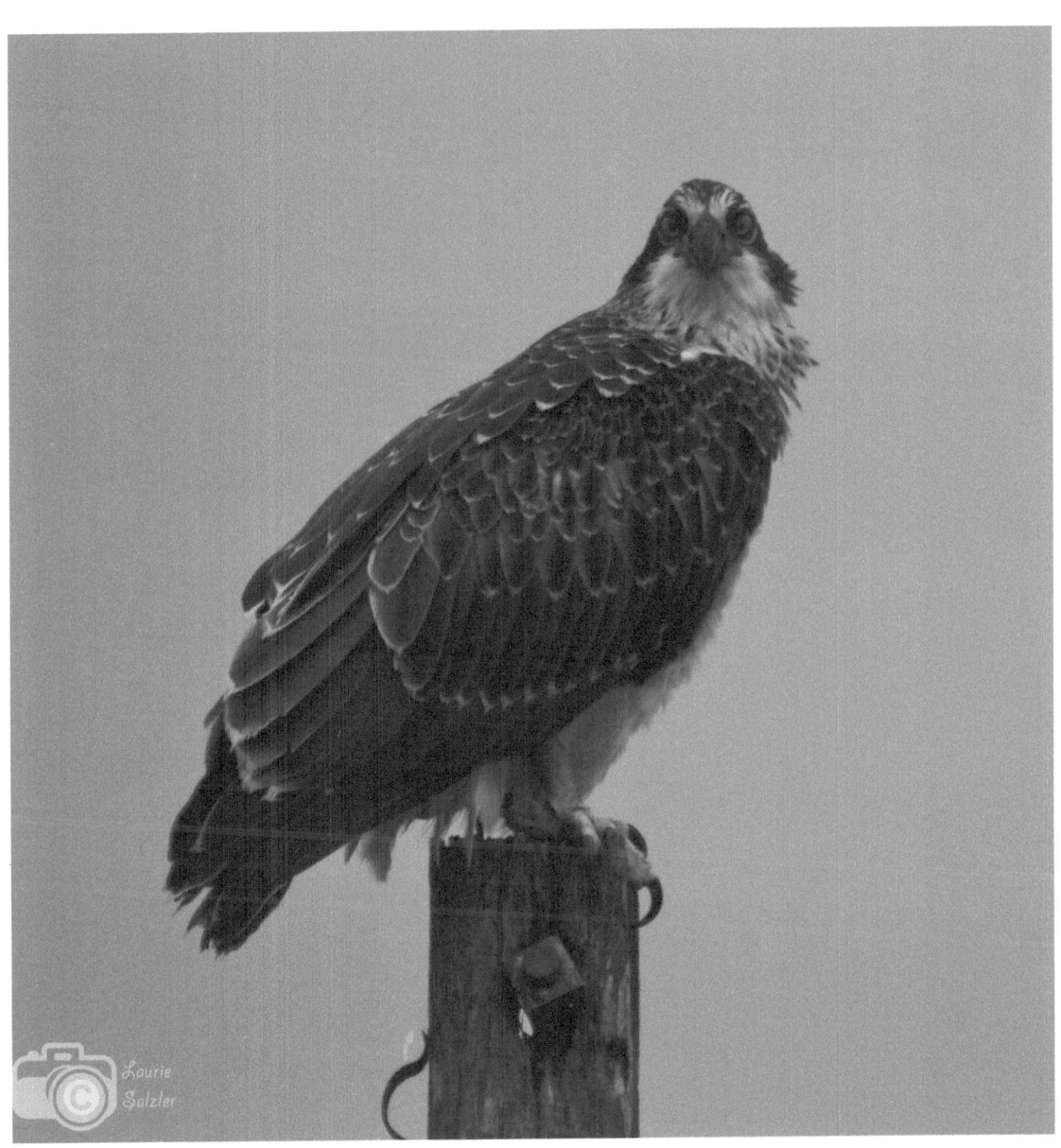

Eastern Osprey
NSW, Australia

When moments of uncertainty fade and instinct connects,
lean out side, lean toward sure,
and take flight, complete the circuit of energy.
It is nature's necessity learned through chance and repetition.
Today is the day.

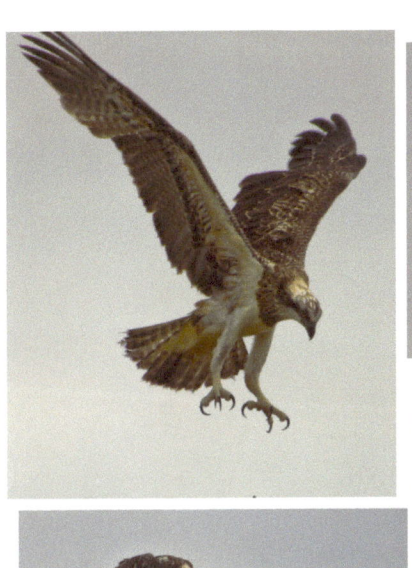
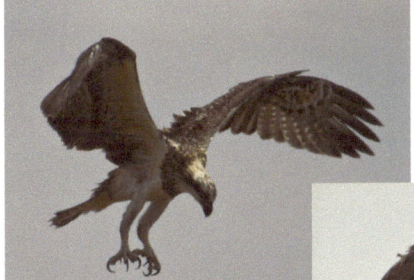
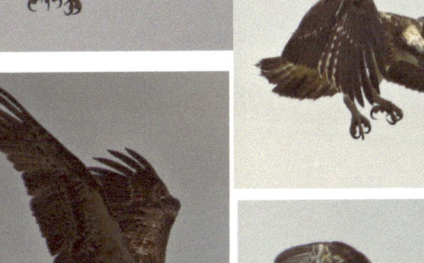
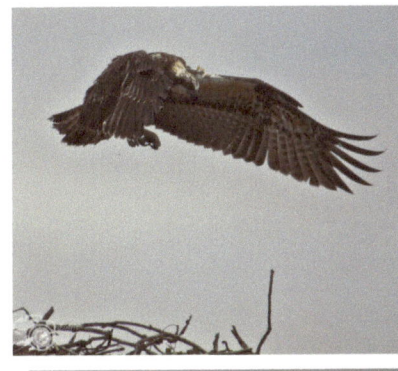
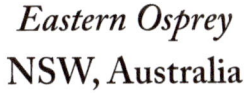
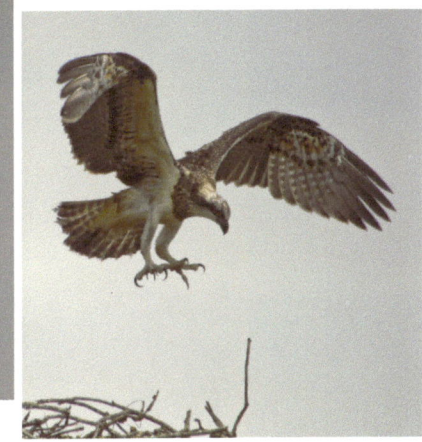

Eastern Osprey
NSW, Australia

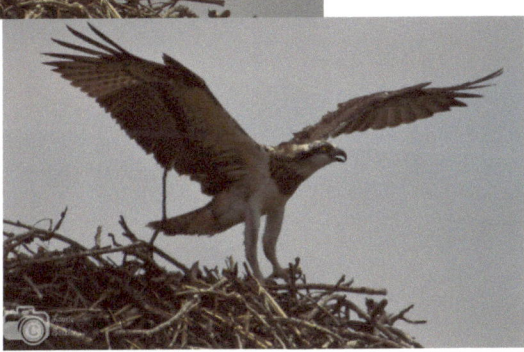
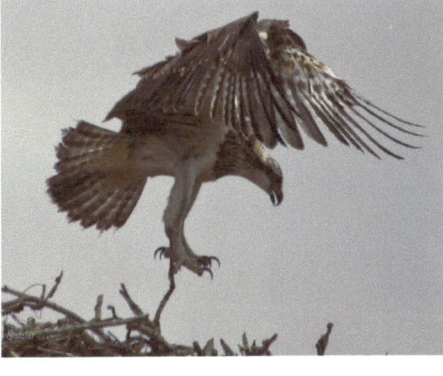

Near the fence, at the far end of the pasture, the palette is filled with Paint.

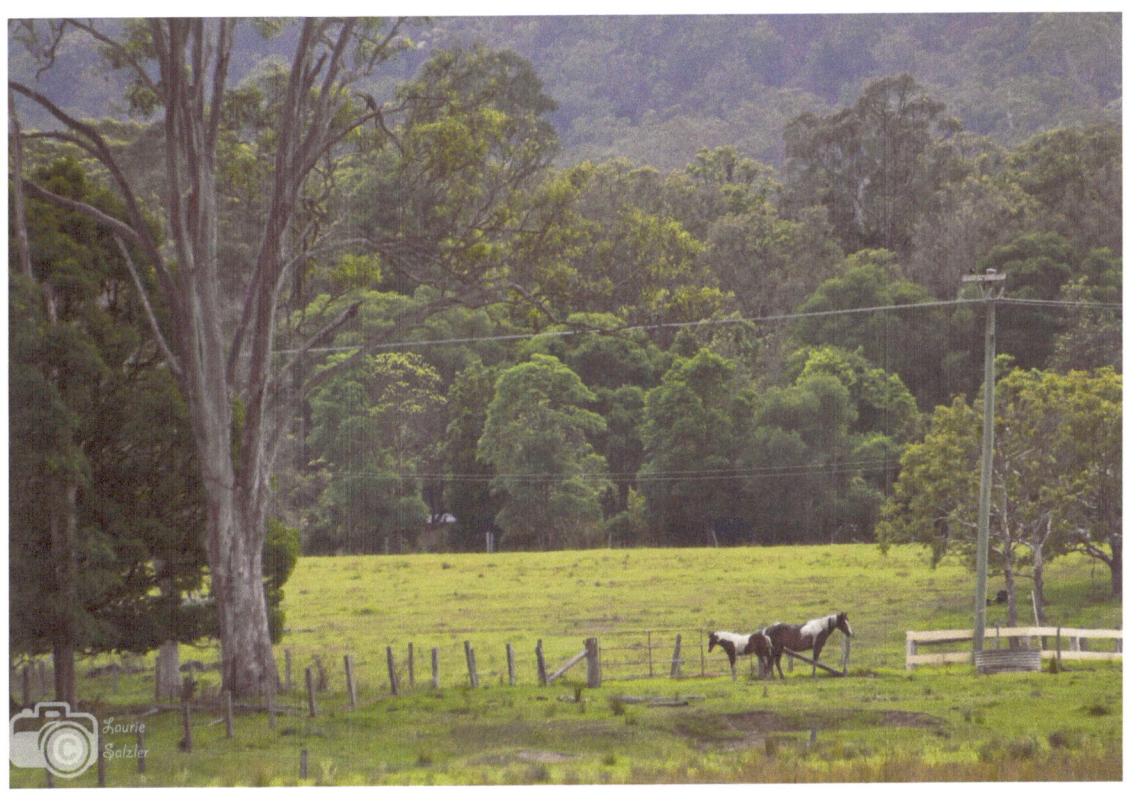

NSW, Australia

There is always a simple yet elegant design,
a complex union of function, color, shape
that combine for another of nature's exquisite gifts.

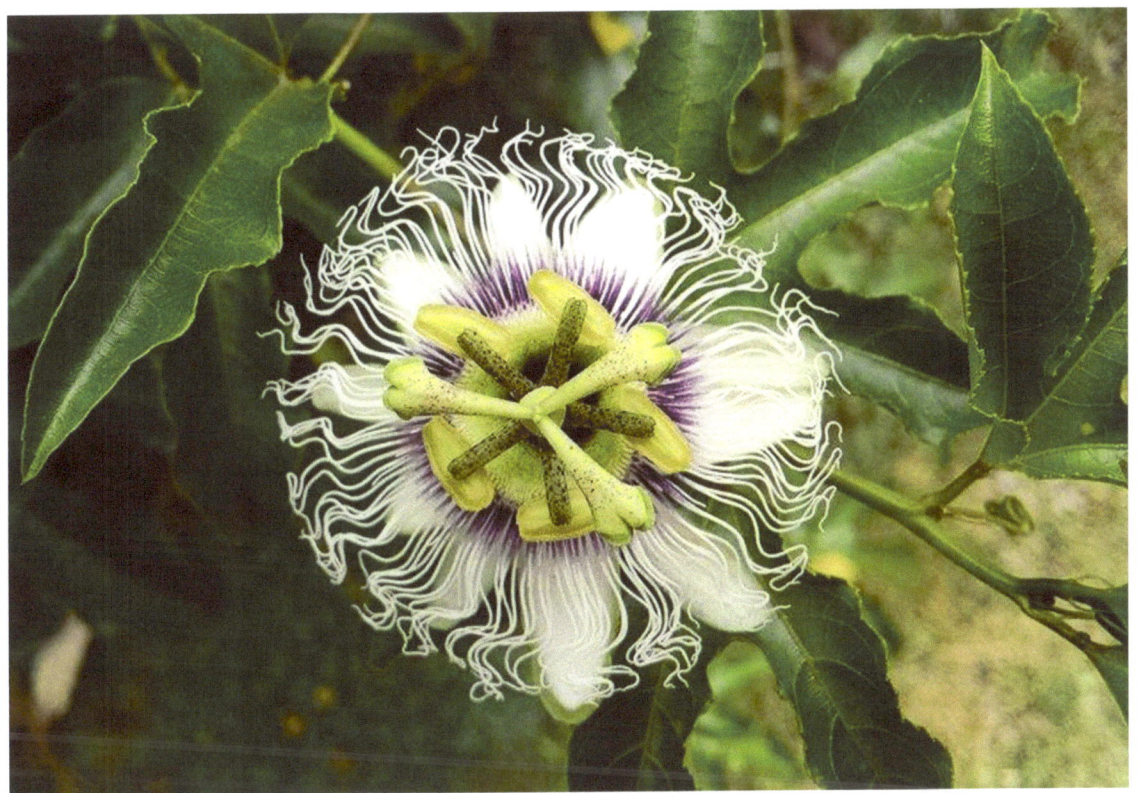

Passionfruit Flower

Before the blushing golden dawn,
before the day's yellow sun,
there is the lavender haze of potential.

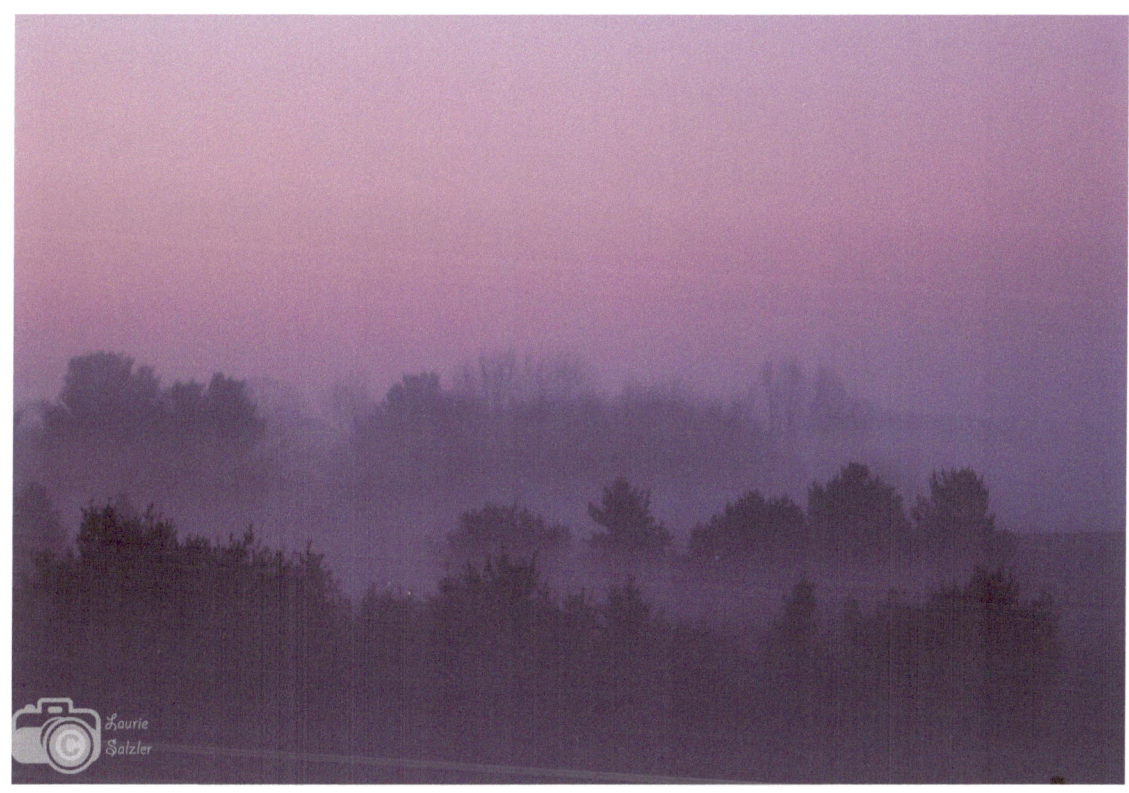

Ann Arbor, Michigan

Gauzing the woods,

plum hue covers all.

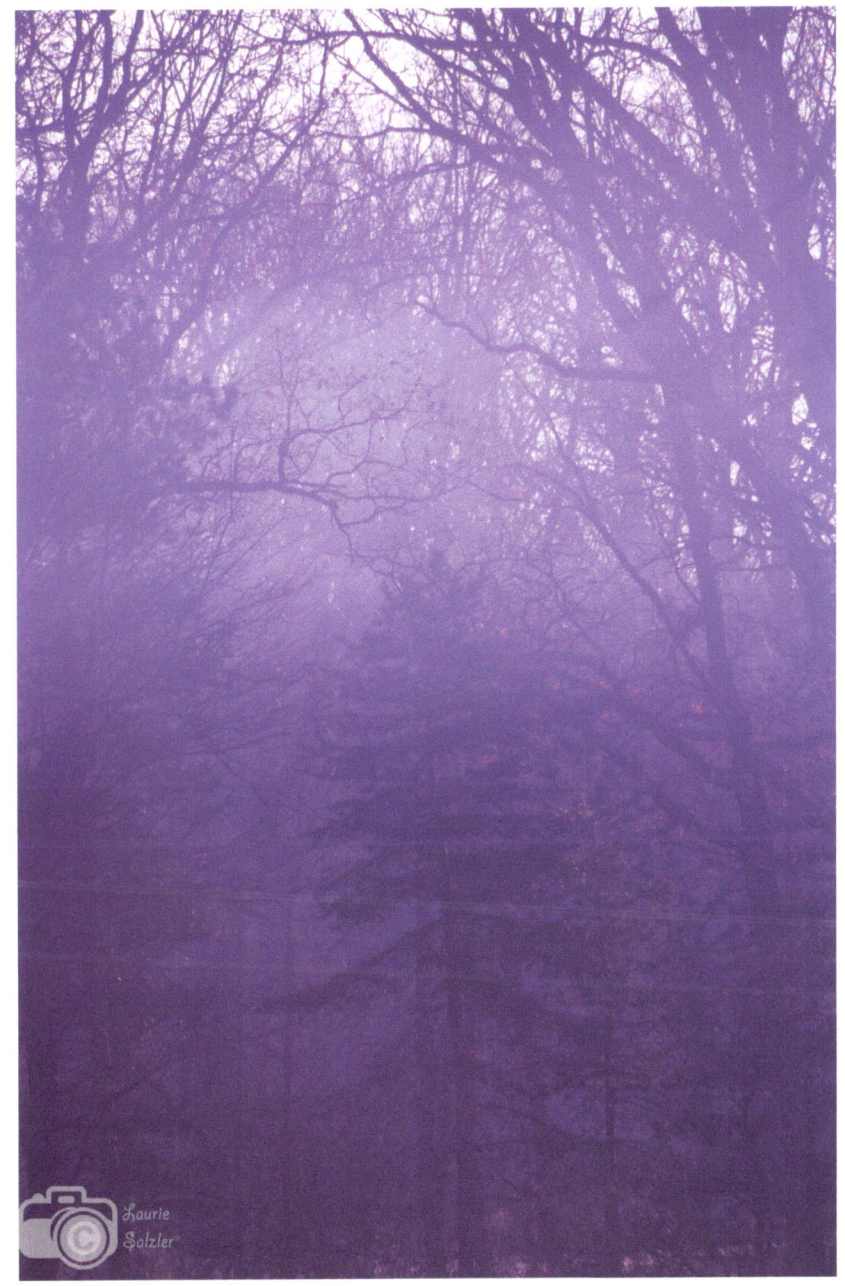

Derby, New York

*The colors opposite,
the intent the same, flying over,
flying to, flying forward.*

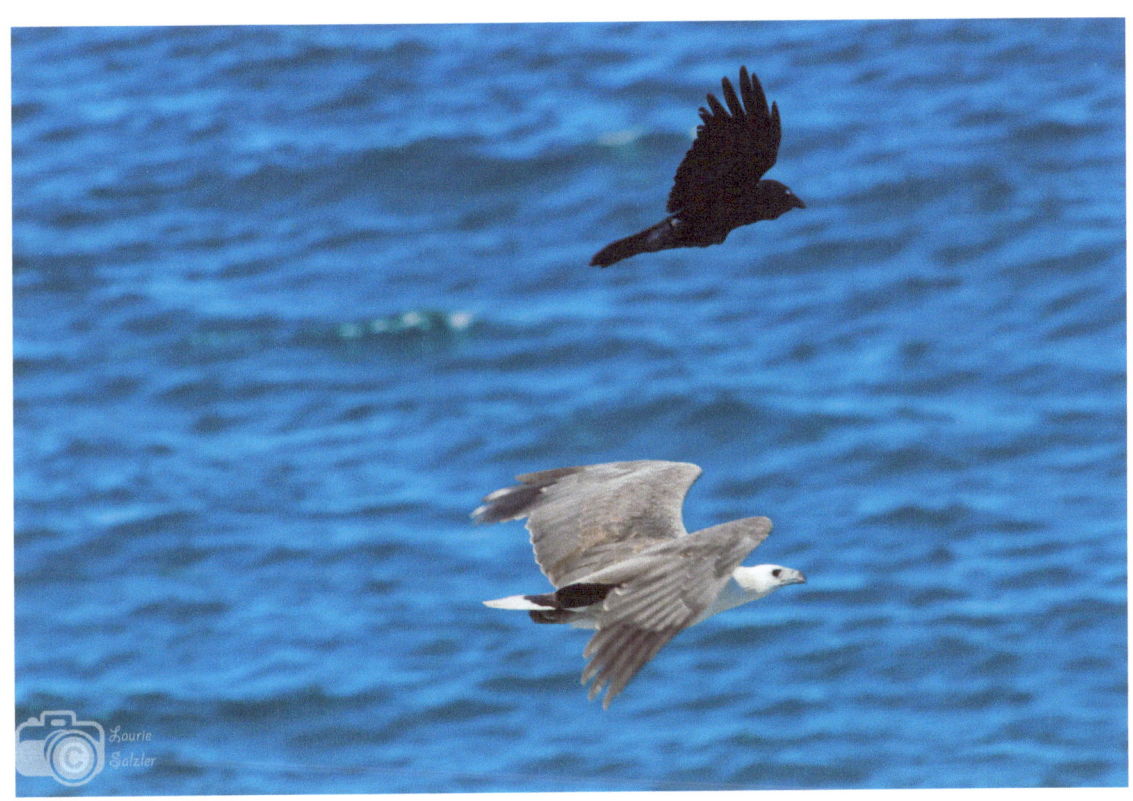

Raven & White-bellied Sea-eagle
Brooms Head, NSW, Australia

No coincidences,
simply desiring the same potential
and the same barkhold with hopes of chiseling
and hammering and finding food.
Winging to the work.

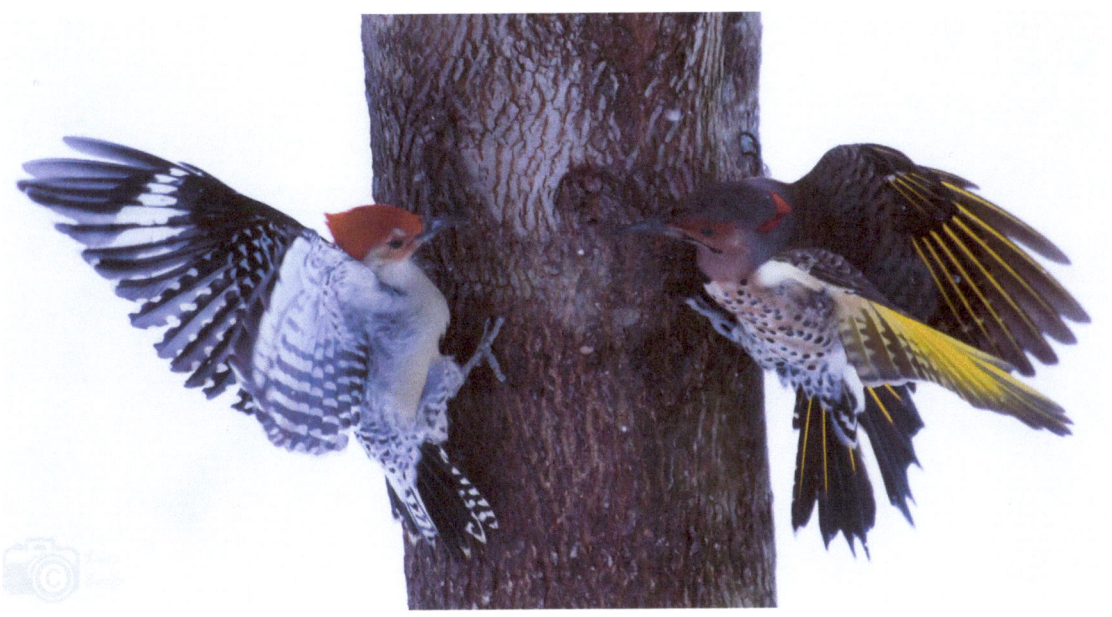

Red-bellied Woodpecker & Flicker

Protected iridescence—
Nature's holiday gold scarab alights,
bringing a luster to the simple green.

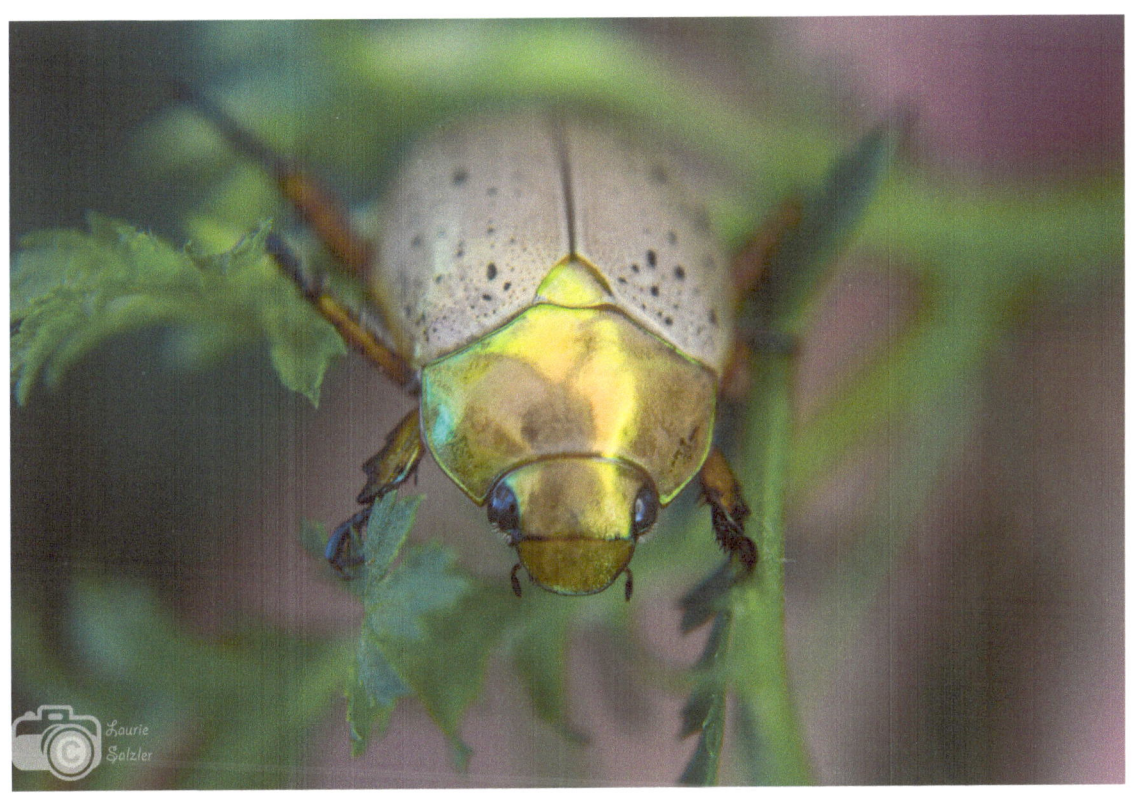

Christmas Beetle
Ashby, NSW, Australia

When the sun has been too long shining,
when the heat of the day takes its toll,
when there is delicious, cool wet mud,
the result is obvious, and absolutely perfect!

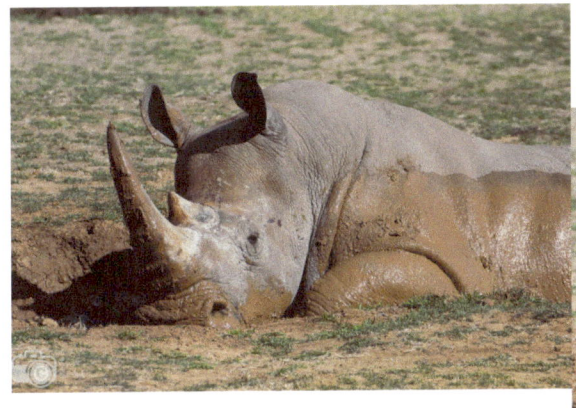
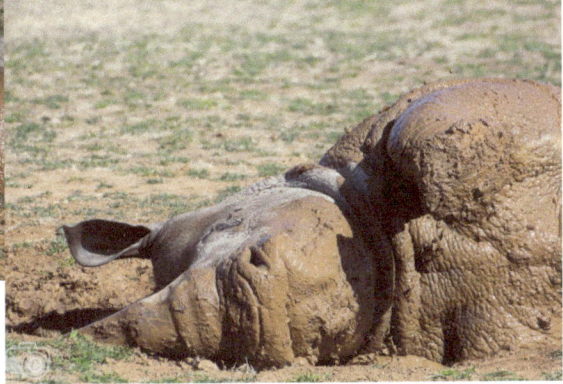
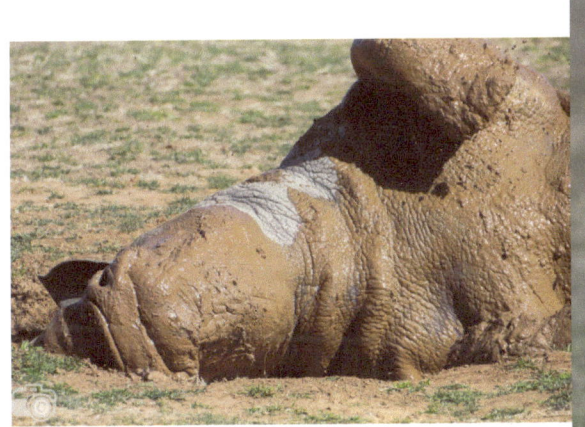
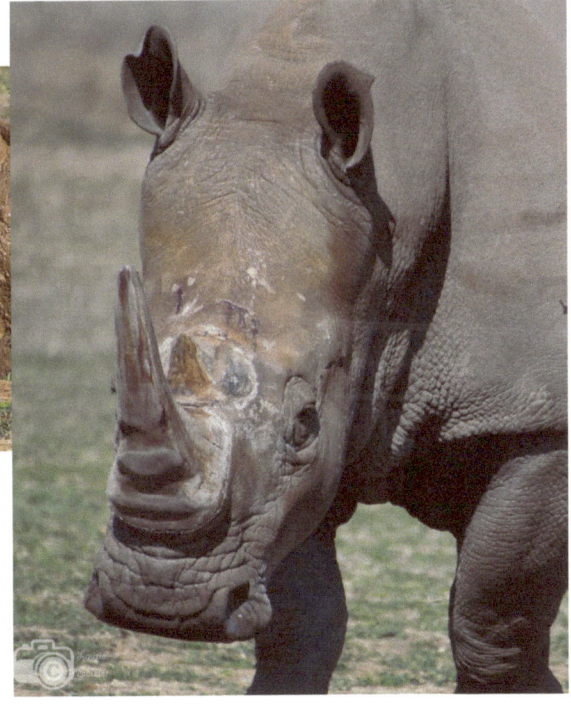

White Rhino
Fossil Rim, Texas

*Bringing a vivid light to any corner,
myriad colors festoon the bushes
and make rainbows redundant.*

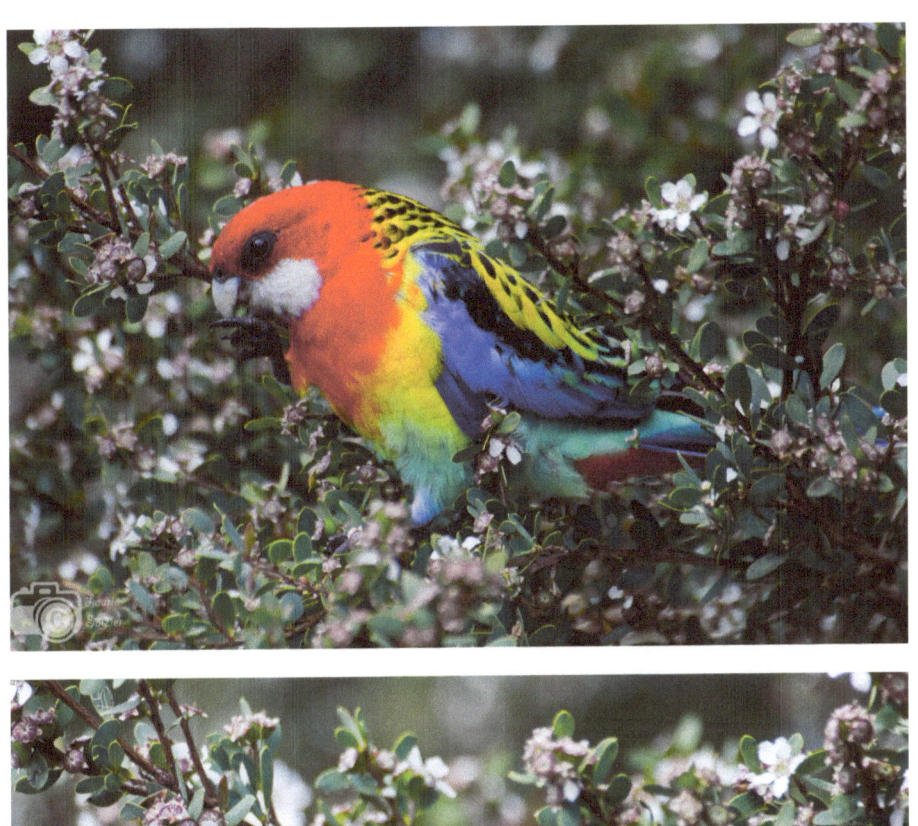

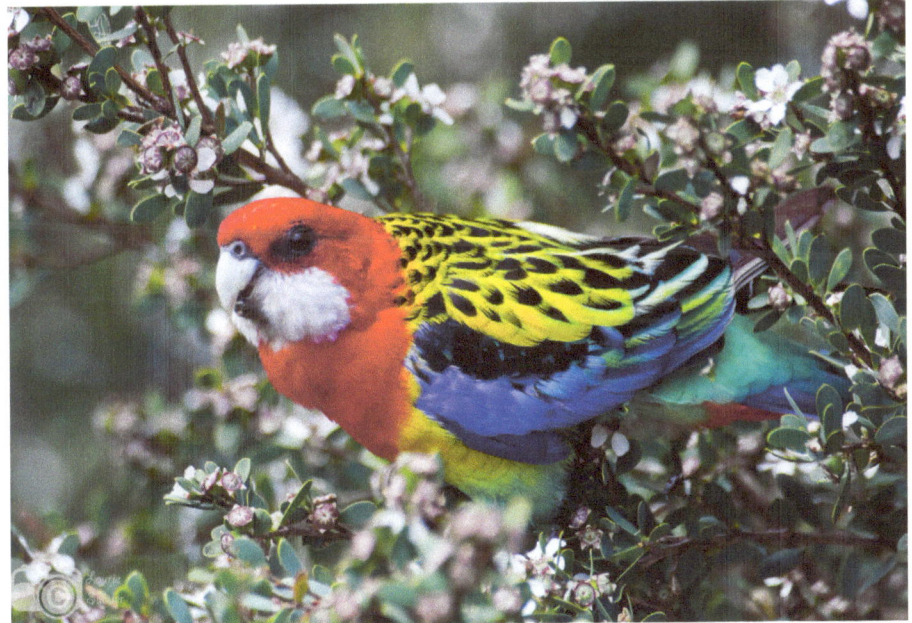

Rosella
Brunswick, NSW, Australia

*Blending in so well,
sometimes it is only by the sounds made
and the songs sung that there is discovery.*

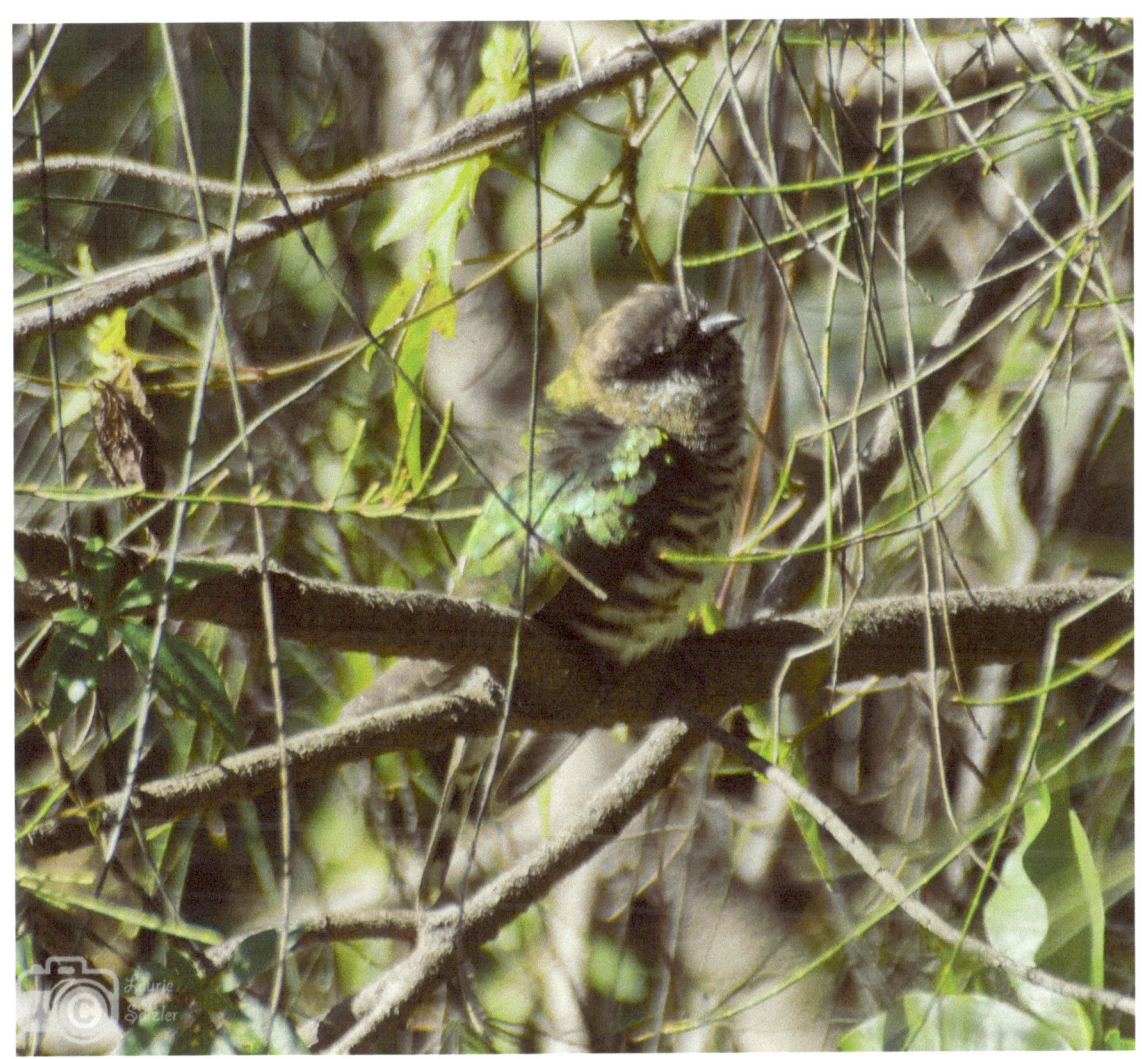

Shining Bronze Cuckoo
Ashby, NSW, Australia

There is perfection in the silent flight,

in the moment of seeing,

in the reality of a split second.

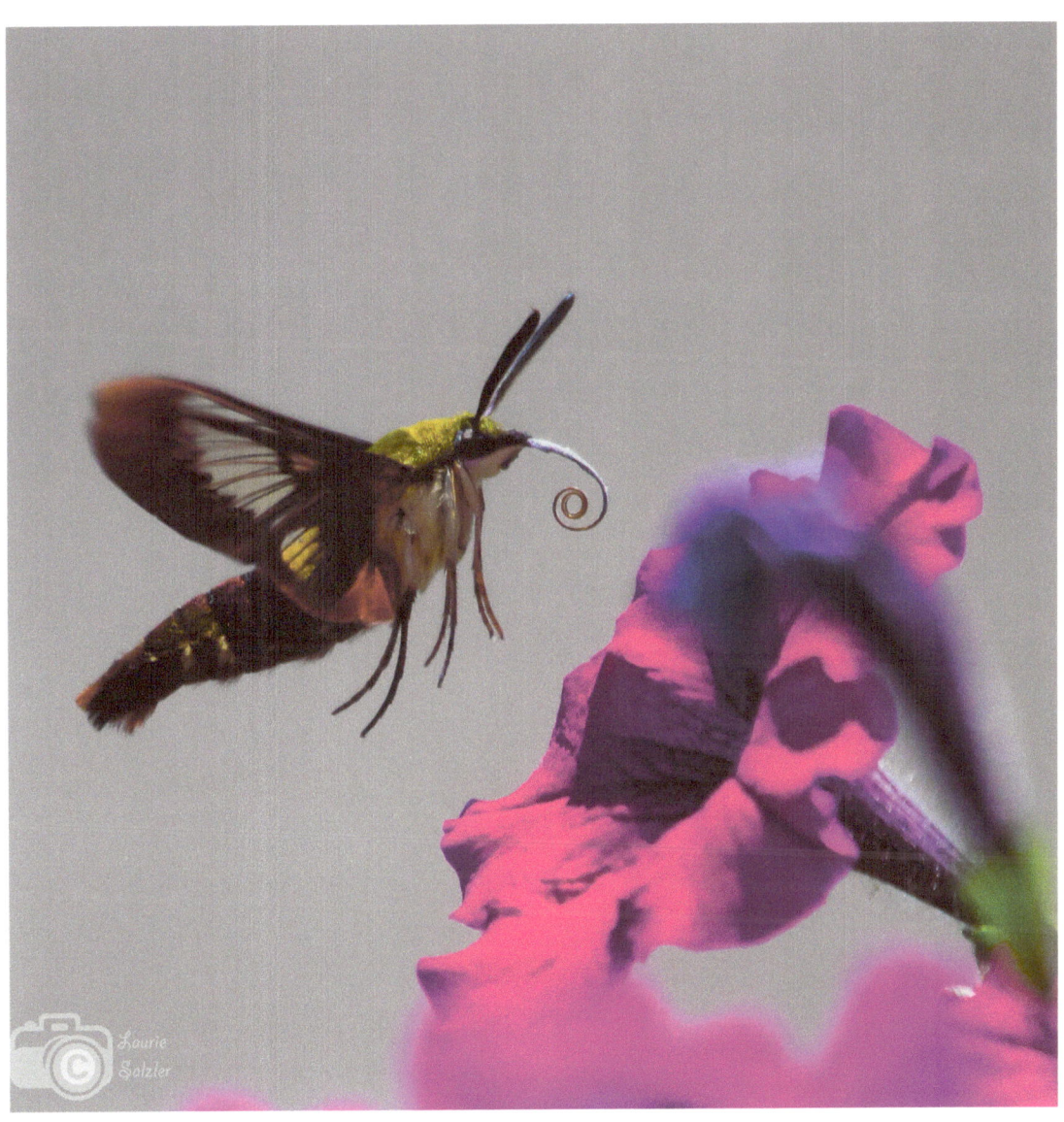

Sphinx Moth
Ann Arbor, Michigan

When there is the presentation of water,
an offering of a soak or a splash or a drink,
flocks descend and the giver enjoys the benefits of the gift.
Harmony.

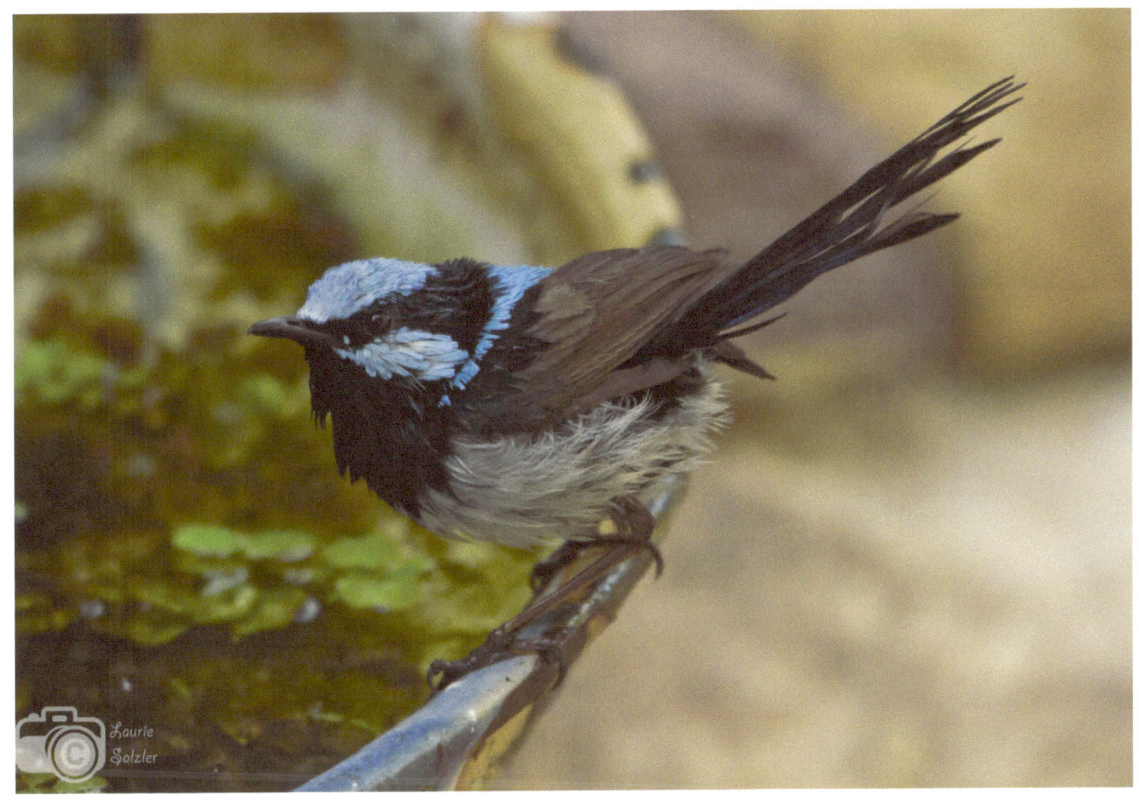

Superb Fairywren
Ashby, NSW, Australia

In shadows,

in silhouette,

inquisitive movements take on a softness mirrored in intention.

Seeing what is not seen

and being among rather than outside, an honest observer.

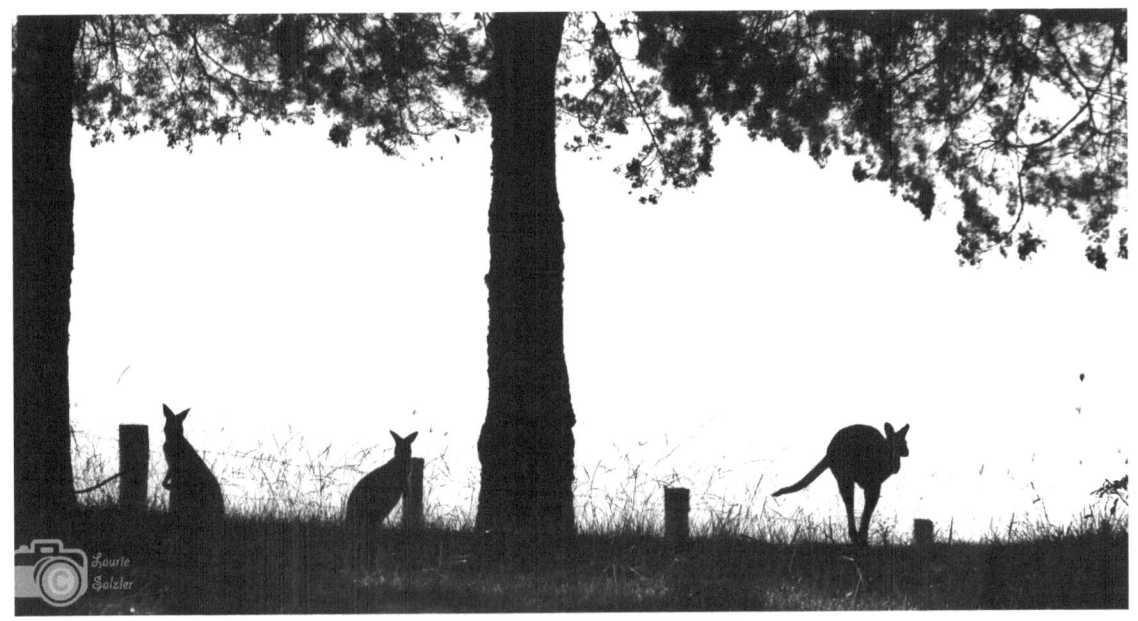

Wallaby Field
Ashby, NSW, Australia

With purpose, poise, and direction all things are possible.

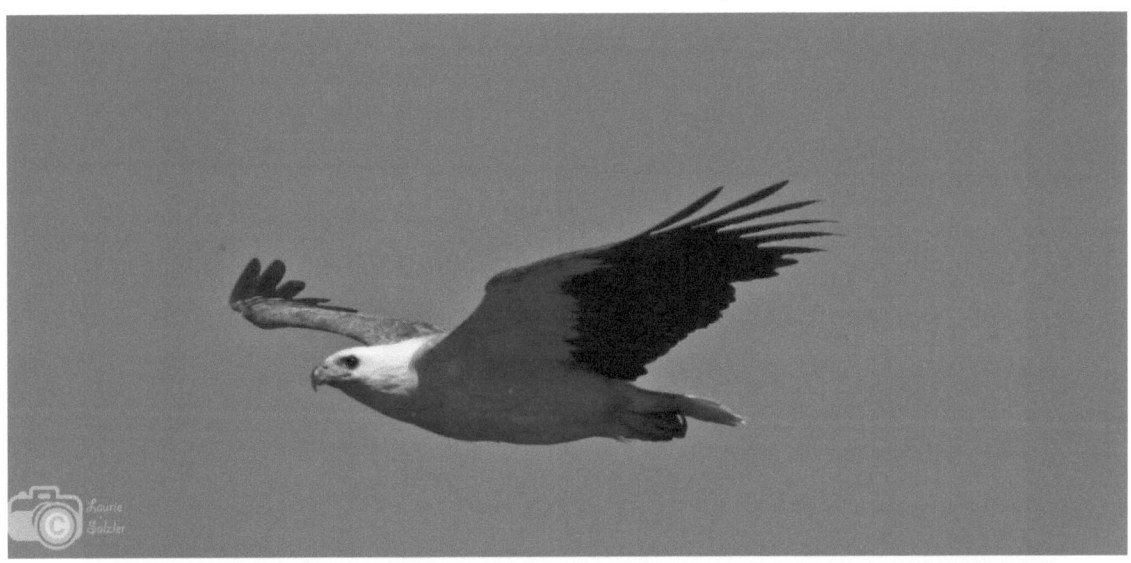

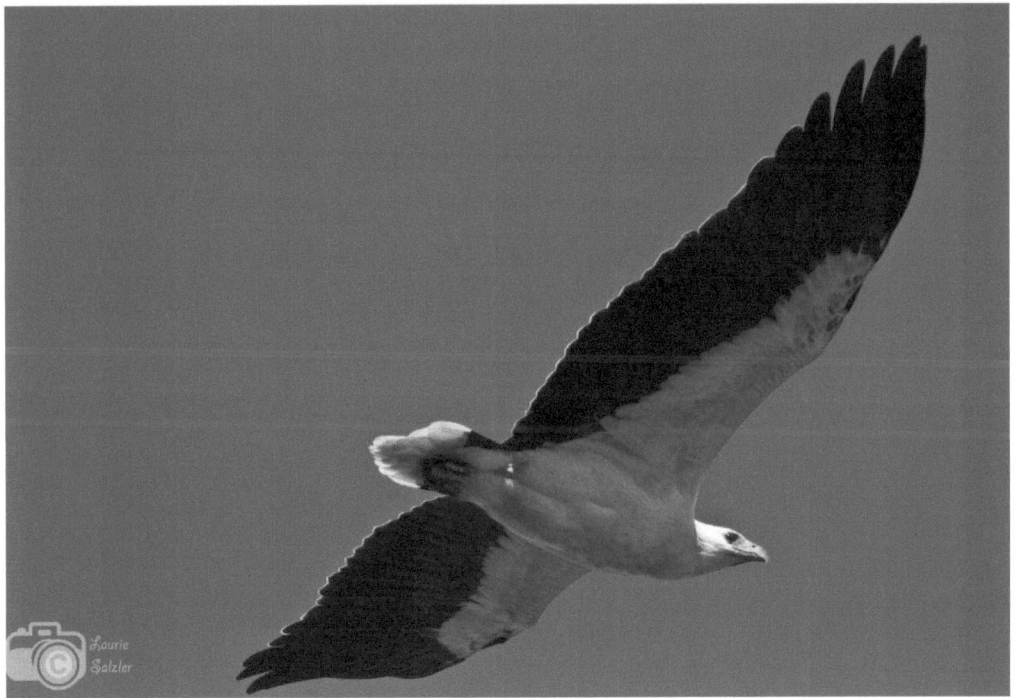

White-bellied Sea-eagle
Ashby, NSW, Australia

No one can know the exact right time for another.

No one can anticipate the ability to leave the comfortable,

to trust the sky.

But by trying,

by spreading wings and taking a chance,

by stepping off—indeed we may soar!

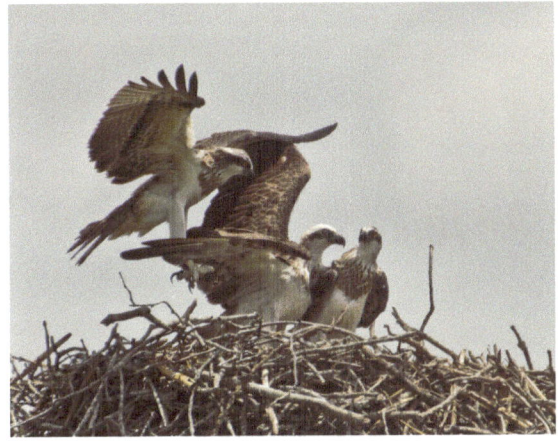
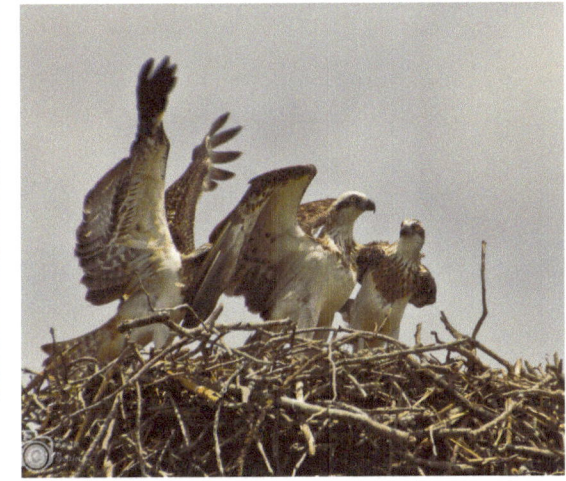
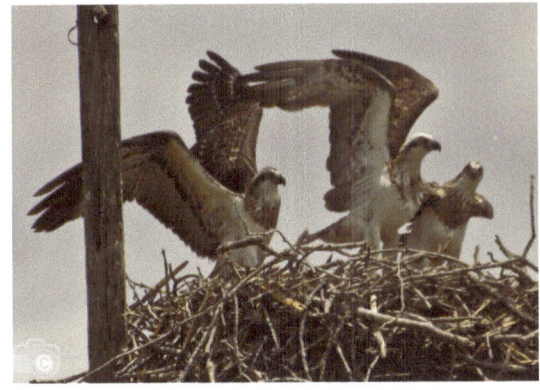
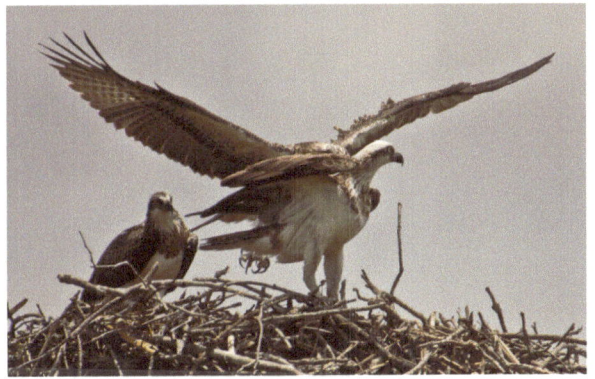

Eastern Osprey
NSW, Australia

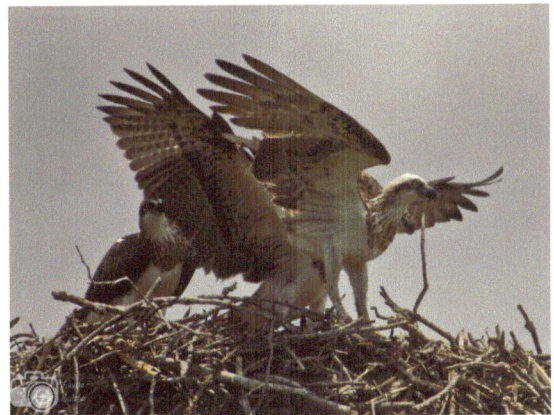
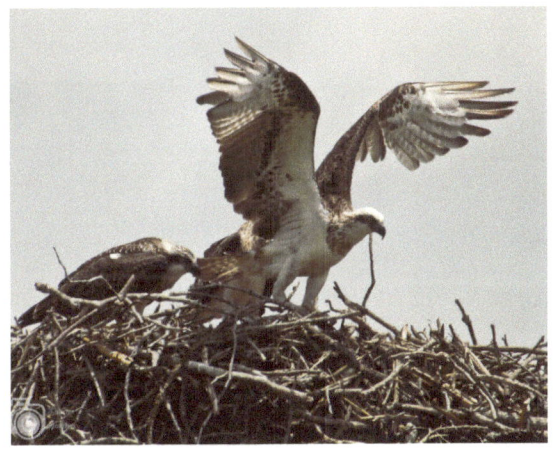

*It is the mesmerizing water,

the movement, the sureness,

the power and the calm—it transcends the wave and the tide,

and offers a peaceful respite.

Endless beginnings*

Eye of the Beholder 133

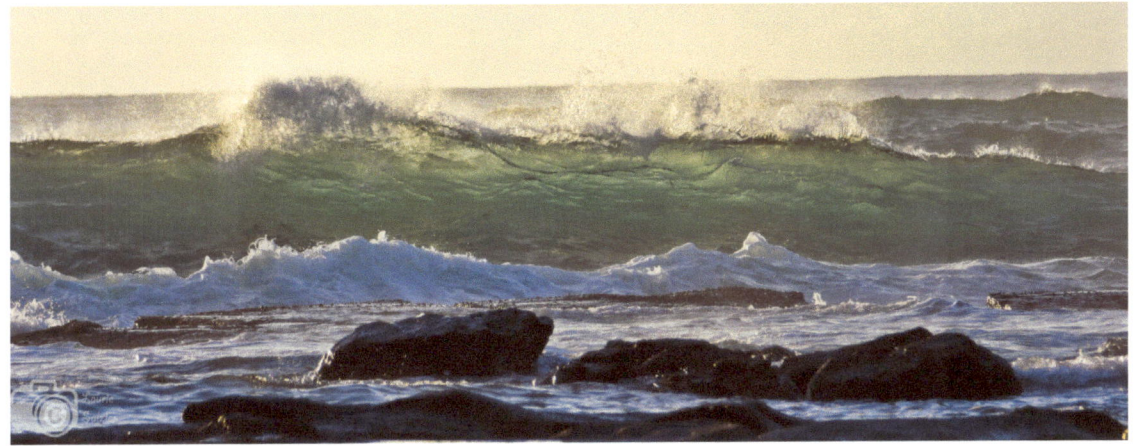

Woody Head, Iluka
NSW, Australia

Looking out, speaking up,

being at ease

and sure makes the most ungainly beautifully elegant.

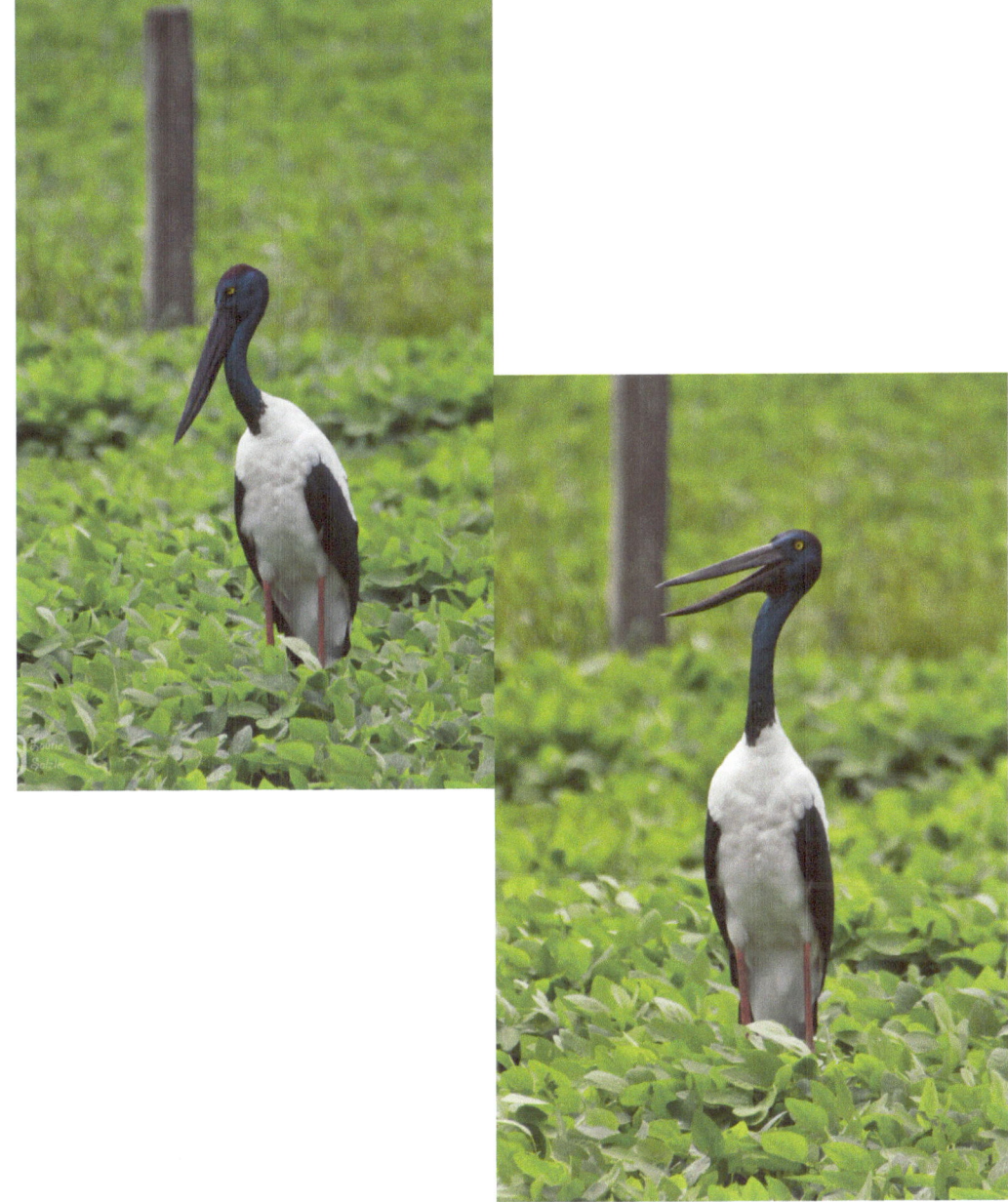

Black-necked Stork
NSW, Australia

In the end, it is perspective.

Lying low and looking up sometimes gives the most advantage,

makes the biggest impact

and the element of surprise serves very well.

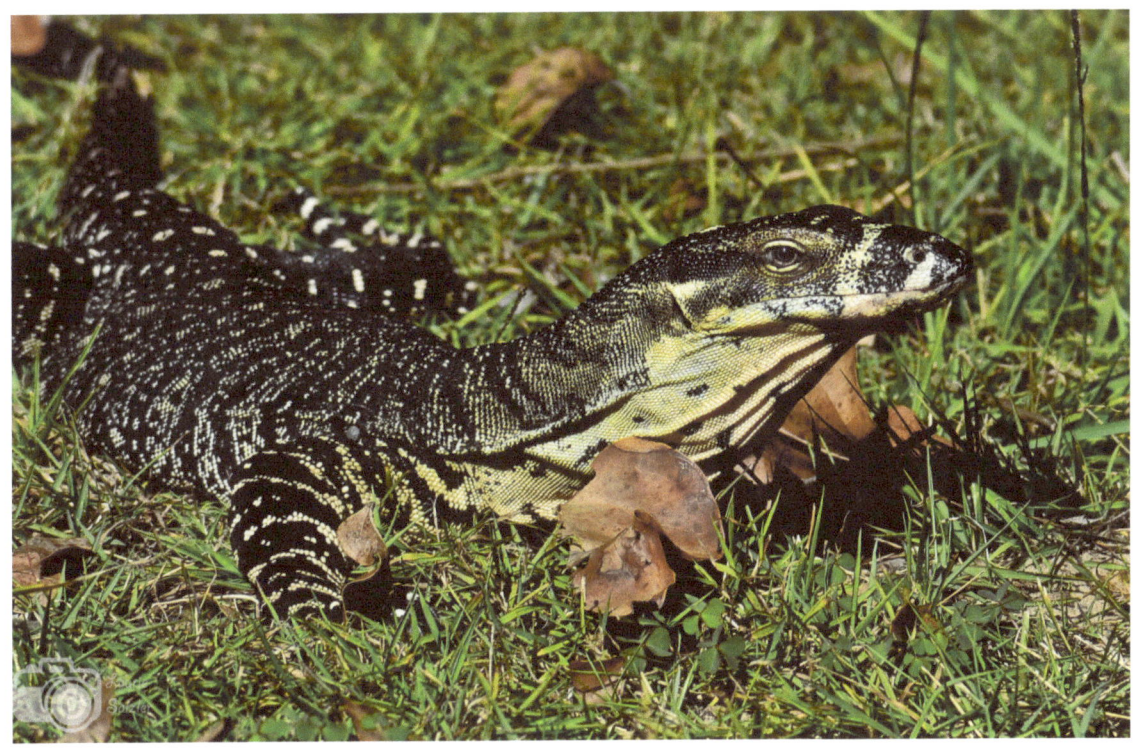

Goanna, Iluka
NSW, Australia

Laurie Salzler

The outdoors and animals, domestic or wildlife, have always been a refuge of sorts for Laurie. Although both play dramatic "characters" in her novels, her photos give the viewer some insight as to the type of woman she is. She often comments that if her work could make one person per day take more notice of the environment and wildlife, this earth may have a better chance at survival.

Originally from a rural farming town in western New York, her travels have taken her far from her birth home over the years. But whether in the woods, on a beach, or in the bush of Australia, and accompanied by her two canine companions, Leika & Kalie, she is truly home.

Sheila Pearsons

Growing up in Michigan, the lakes, streams, beaches and wooded paths offered the best learning for Sheila Pearsons. More formal education resulted in a BA in English, MA in Modern American Lit, and a Master's degree in Library Science, but the outdoors has always been the most welcome teacher. For more than 30 years, Sheila was a Librarian with the Bay County Library System, retiring in 2010. Since then, flyfishing, wordworks, golf, walking, snowshoeing, reading, and watercolor dabbling have occupied many of the days. Hours spent on the beach, wading the rivers and collecting words have made for a happy third chapter in a most grateful life.

www.ingramcontent.com/pod-product-compliance
Lightning Source LLC
Chambersburg PA
CBHW051148220526
45473CB00003B/704